STANDING ON HOLY GROUND

STANDING ON HOLY GROUND

by Robert Nash, S.J.

NP

The Newman Press · Westminster, Maryland

1955

←⋘ He Passed This Way

De Licentia Superiorum Ordinis: Michael O'Grady, S.J.
Praep. Prov. Hib. Soc. Jesu

Nihil Obstat: Edward A. Cerny, S.S., D.D., *Censor librorum*

Imprimatur: Most Reverend Francis P. Keough, D.D., *Archbishop of Baltimore*

September 9, 1955

Library of Congress Catalog Card Number: 55-12010

Dedicated to

SAINT IGNATIUS LOYOLA
IN HIS QUADRICENTENNIAL YEAR

Foreword

These chapters appeared originally as a series in a Dublin daily, *The Irish Press*. By courtesy of the editor they are now being published in book form, having been expanded and completely rewritten. Thirty-eight pilgrims, nearly all Irish, left Dublin by plane on October 28, 1954, for the Holy Land; this little volume is an attempt to put into words some of their experiences.

While the articles were going through the press, Mr. Christopher Hollis, a Catholic member of Parliament in England, went on television and spoke about "the scandal of the Holy Places." He describes Nazareth as "the leading city of Communism in Israel." While we were in Nazareth we were told that the Communists won the last election there "by an overwhelming majority." At the same time, it is worth recording the assurance we were given by a Catholic Arab married man at Nazareth. He denied that at heart the town was Communist, and dwelt on the willingness of the people to work for the Church whenever an appeal was made. "It would be far more difficult," says Mr. Hollis, "for Mary and Joseph to make the journey from Nazareth to Bethlehem today than it would have been in the time of the Emperor Augustus," for "one of the most bloody of the recent

Arab-Israel clashes took place in what is virtually a suburb of Bethlehem."

He speaks of the shocking condition of the Church of the Holy Sepulchre in Jerusalem which would seem to be almost ready to fall down owing to Christian neglect. Repairs can be carried out only on condition that all the Christian bodies contribute each their share in defraying the necessary expenses. The Greek Orthodox are not able to pay and will not consent to allow the rest to bear the whole cost. Hence the present impasse which can hardly be to the credit of Christians in the eyes of the world.

That these bitter complaints are only too well justified is painfully evident to those privileged to go in pilgrimage to the country of Our Lord. Mr. Hollis suggests that the problem be solved by internationalizing the Holy Places. The disgraceful state of affairs has arisen and continues "because so few people throughout the Christian world take any interest in it or care in the least that it should be solved." The Church of the Holy Sepulchre is held together by a temporary scaffolding erected by the British Royal Engineers nearly thirty years ago, and when a recent earthquake cracked the roof, the repairs were carried out by King Abdulla, a Moslem, "simply because there was no chance that if left to the Christians it would ever be done at all."

In proposing internationalization, Mr. Hollis is supporting the solution already recommended many times by the Holy See. Since the division of the country in 1948, Pope Pius XII has pleaded for the application of this remedy, and even before him the United Nations Organization had advocated it and approved of it. But it has not been applied, either because the disputing parties could not agree, or because certain groups, for selfish reasons, brought pressure to bear and succeeded in keeping the breach open.

The Pope's pronouncements were pushed into the background, and later some sections of the world press declared that the Holy See had changed its mind concerning the advantages of internationalization, and was now of opinion that the present state of affairs should be accepted.

This statement was met by the Vatican by a vigorous denial. The view of the Holy Father remained unchanged and the Pontiff regards the position as "sad, precarious, and dangerous," and considers that the present boundary line is held by brute force and not by reasoned judgment. Apart altogether from moral considerations of justice and charity, any sincere desire for lasting peace in Palestine must seek to bring about the ending of unrest, so prevalent there at the moment.

Equally outspoken are the Pope's words about the hundreds of thousands of Arab refugees who have fled from their homes and are still living in camps in Syria and Egypt, in Jordan, the Lebanon, and in Israel. This problem too, says the Vatican *Osservatore Romano*, must be tackled and solved in accordance with the principles of justice, without which there can be no lasting peace.

In the following pages we have prescinded almost entirely from mention of these acute problems. We have underlined, rather, the sacredness of the spots consecrated by the events of Our divine Lord's life, and the effects which intimate contact with them must make if they are visited in the spirit of faith. Emphasis of this aspect may prove to be a modest contribution to offset the challenge made by Mr. Hollis. It may even bring the voice and the appeal of the Holy Father to ears which either have not heard it before, or having heard, have not been sufficiently alert to the urgency of the message.

ROBERT NASH, S.J.

Rathfarnham Castle, Dublin.
Feast of Epiphany, January 6, 1955.

Acknowledgments

We wish to thank the following publishers for permission to quote from copyrighted works:

Mr. Basil Clancy, publisher of the Irish magazine, *Hibernia;*

Harcourt, Brace and Company, Inc., publishers of *The Pillar of Fire* by Karl Stern;

The Macmillan Company, publishers of *The Glory of Thy People* by M. Raphael Simon, O.C.S.O.;

David McKay Company, Inc., publishers of *Star of Jacob* by Helen Walker Homan;

The Society for Promoting Christian Knowledge, publishers of *The Jewish People and Jesus Christ* by Jacob Jocz.

Contents

Illustrations

The illustrations in the text were furnished through the courtesy of the Embassy of Israel, Washington, D. C.

STANDING ON HOLY GROUND

1 . *He Passed This Way*

A priest dropped in to see me. Both of us were in Jerusalem, members of a group of pilgrims from Ireland. "I'm going to admit," he said, "that this is an overpowering experience. Don't you feel awe-inspired when you stand here before the altar for Mass and think to yourself: 'This is the very spot. He was crucified here, for my sins. Mary stood here beside the cross, right where I am standing now.' On every side it's the same. The atmosphere is charged with the clinging memory of what He did and what He said and how He said it, in these precise places where you and I find ourselves at this moment. I'm all the while thinking: He was here; He looked down along those streets and walked barefoot over those cobblestones; He climbed this mountain and knelt here to pray."

Most pilgrims will agree. The Holy Land definitely does something to you. A few days earlier I had driven in from the airport and got my first glimpse of this city seated upon a hill. The sight rather repels you at first, for the hill is arid and stony, with scarce a blade of grass to be seen, and you tell yourself that its forbidding aspect accords well with the crime forever linked inseparably to its name. For this is the hill upon which men raised a gibbet to crucify their Saviour; its very barrenness seems to broadcast to the world the story of the great rejection. "Get away from Jerusalem as soon as you can," a friend had advised me before leaving home, "and spend as much time as possible by the Sea of Galilee."

In another place we shall talk about the charm and the wonders of that Sea.

WHERE AM I?

But in fairness to Jerusalem it must be stated that if your first reactions are unfavorable, presently they undergo a profound change. As we jogged along and I was musing and observing, presently the voice of our driver broke in on my reflections. "If you look over there, about half a mile to your left, you can see the Garden of Gethsemani and the Church of the Agony. Right behind the Church, on both sides, stretches the Valley of Cedron topped by the Mount of Olivet from which Christ ascended into heaven. Halfway up the slope you have the place where He sat and wept over Jerusalem, and, below, at His feet, you see the site of what was then the magnificent Temple. It's a mosque now, called the Mosque of Omar. We're getting into the city itself. That Church?

It's the Church of the Holy Sepulchre, which contains the place where Christ was crucified and buried, and whence He rose again after His death."

It is impossible to convey in cold print the effect words like these have on your innermost soul. Is it all a dream, you wonder, or is it sober reality that you are finding yourself, literally, following in His very footsteps? Are these the very streets that re-echoed to the sound of His voice, as one time He pleaded with men to seek their happiness in the love of His Sacred Heart, or again spoke words of stern and uncompromising condemnation of their sins, or of warning to repent while yet there was time?

In this alone lies the all-absorbing interest for the true pilgrim to the Holy Land—that here is the place where the Son of God was born and lived and ate and slept and worked and preached and prayed; this is the ground sanctified by the treading of His feet; this is the scene of His miracles, where He multiplied the loaves and fishes or raised the dead to life or cleansed the lepers or gave sight to the blind. This is the place where words bearing inexpressible consolation to sinners were spoken, where He invited all who are weary and who labor and are burdened to come to Him and be assured of rest to their souls. Along this way He walked to Calvary bearing His own cross, stressing by His own example the truth He had already enunciated, that unless a man be prepared to carry his cross he cannot follow in the steps of his Master and Lord. In this very place, quite close to that cross of Christ, stood Mary His Mother, watching and uniting with Him in making the supreme sacrifice.

GET AT REALITY

In view of truths like these who is so foolish as to waste time wrangling over dates or exact sites? How can anybody have eyes for structures made by the hands of man, how splendid soever they may be as monuments of love and faith? Deeper than all is embedded the basic fact that Jesus passed this way, and on that satisfying truth the pilgrim wants to feed his hungering soul. All other interests here, and beyond question there are many, can hold the attention only in passing. They are mere accidental trappings. The substantial fare for which the soul craves is the realization that the ground beneath one's feet is holy ground.

Moses on the mountain saw a bush which, though on fire, was not burning up. Prompted by what might fairly be considered as pardonable curiosity he drew near to investigate this strange phenomenon. "And when the Lord saw that he went forward to see, he called to him out of the midst of the bush, and said: Moses, Moses. And he answered: Here I am. And he said: Come not nigh hither. Put off the shoes from thy feet, for the place whereon thou standest is holy ground" (Exod. 3:4–5).

There is a little word of three letters which everywhere in this Holy Land hits you in the eye. It is the Latin word *hic*, meaning "here." It speaks volumes and provides material for a lifetime of prayer and meditation. You go into the Church of the Annunciation at Nazareth and kneel at the hallowed spot of the mystery. "*Verbum caro HIC factum est*," you read. "The word was HERE made flesh." Mary knelt HERE and HERE Gabriel stood and executed his sacred commission. Down at Bethlehem you come to do homage and once again there is the significant message: "*Christus HIC natus est*"; "Christ was born HERE." At Calvary and in its precincts you are reminded: "*HIC flagellatus est; HIC coronatus; HIC crucifixus, mortuus, et sepultus . . .*" "THIS is the very place where He was crowned with thorns, scourged, and nailed to the cross; HERE He died and HERE He was buried . . ."

We met a group of women in Jaffa who had travelled long distances in order to visit the graves of their husbands, all killed in the war. That does not surprise one; human nature is like that, for love clings to whatever has any association with the person loved —a house, a book, a letter, a photo. *Hic*, here, *He* was born and lived and worked and suffered and died. The pilgrim goes to Jerusalem and the Holy Places because he would drink deep at the fountains of divine love and not thirst forever. If this Holy Land does something to you, it is to help you to taste and to see for yourself that the Lord is sweet. The story written across its streets and its hills and valleys, the story leaping up from the waters of its lakes and rivers, mirrored in its blue skies and reflected in its brilliant sunshine, is the tale of the divine romance, ever ancient, ever new, telling how God so loved the world as to give His only-begotten Son. And HERE is where it all happened.

WHY WE CAME

On my first night in Jerusalem I went down with a friend by the Via Dolorosa into the Garden of Gethsemani. You felt, indeed, that like Moses you should cast the shoes from off your feet. The crowds jostled noisily along this route, the very road He had walked bearing His own cross. But there is nothing farther from their minds than that journey and the Person Who had made it and for what purpose. Gethsemani, a little outside the city, to the east, lay still in the moonlight, inviting men to come down here and reflect and pray. But do not imagine that it was, on that night, filled with devout worshippers kneeling in spirit with a Christ Who sweated blood and groaned in anguish and loneliness under those olive trees. Not at all. Most people in Jerusalem have forgotten all that, even if they ever knew.

There are those who will ask: "Why go to the Holy Land? Haven't we all it can give in our tabernacles and on our altars at home?" Yes and no. We have, indeed, the same Christ and the same Sacrifice. But, for those privileged to visit the Holy Places the veil enshrouding those mysteries is drawn aside, be it ever so little, and faith is deepened and love is made stronger, and to the pilgrim new zest is imparted, on returning home, to tell the world what he has seen and heard and experienced HERE.

It is not mere intellectual conviction that fills and satisfies the soul. There is also the spirit of faith which breathes new life into divine truth and makes it a reality. It is doubtful if there is any atmosphere where one so quickly and so naturally senses the supernatural as one does here. That is one reason why the urge is strong to bring as many others as possible to the knowledge and love of Him Who passed this way.

2. *Meeting the Arabs*

The window of my room overlooked an Arab street. Palestine has been divided, since 1948, into two sections: Jordan, which is inhabited exclusively by Arabs, and Israel, with something more than one million Jews and about a hundred and seventy thousand Arabs. We began our pilgrimage in Jordan, a section including a large portion of Old Jerusalem and many of the Holy Places.

May I ask you to imagine yourself coming out the main door of that hotel and turning sharply to your left? The ugly huge building directly in front of the hotel is the citadel where Pilate used to live when he did not occupy the Palace Antonia in the center of the city. Your turn to the left has brought you into King David Street and we propose to walk along it together. It is extremely narrow, perhaps six feet across, and it is swarming with humanity. Faces pop up in all sorts of unexpected places; shops abound which sell everything from a needle to an anchor, and pilgrims are set upon to buy or even step inside to see the fabulous bargains.

A jovial friend had cheerfully explained to me,

9

before we came away from Dublin, that I might find myself in an Arab street with a knife sticking in my back, or with my throat neatly slit by a knife! At first, indeed, you did feel some uneasiness while making your way along those strange streets, with strange eyes fixed upon you, and at night especially there was an eerie sensation. I like to put this on record because it was to be so completely shattered, as will presently appear, by our actual experience in dealing with these grand people.

BEDLAM!

Jewellers and cloth merchants and chemists and sellers of fish, sweet shops and repositories of religious goods, restaurants and tobacco shops—they are all here, giving the impression of a Babel of confusion and congestion, and seeming to the visitor to be getting hopelessly in each other's hair. You wonder how all of them manage to eke out a living and you surmise that business must be brisk when, at peak periods, pilgrims and tourists throng the city. We were warned repeatedly that they were "sharks." Nobody in his senses, we were told, should entertain the idea of going in to buy, if he did not want to be fleeced, unless accompanied by a reliable guide. Nobody gives any credence to what these zealous men of business sound forth, and that they themselves are the very first to take for granted! "The day the Arab tells the truth will be the end of the world."

Vendors are incredibly persistent. They will keep on following you and try to press their goods into your hand, whether you smile or frown or affect to ignore them, or whether you cry out "Isbish!"—which means, we were told, "Begone!" This is their one chance in life to do business with you, and they need no reminder from you to seize upon it.

You will sometimes be treated to heartrending stories in the hope of softening that hard heart of yours and opening your purse-strings. Three little girls followed me one day in tears, real tears! The tale was that mother was dead, and father had deserted them, and they had nothing at all to eat. Please do not think too unkindly of me when I admit that what I did was to slip my hand into my pocket and produce, not the eagerly-expected "baksheesh," but a pocket handkerchief. I pretended to weep with them, in mock sympathy, holding the handkerchief to my eyes. The effect was electrical! They saw at once that the game was up and instantly the tears disappeared and were replaced by grins of merriment! Isbish!

Still, you insult an Arab if you count the change he gives you. And if you go into his shop and select a few cards he will never count them but assume you have given him the correct number. One of our party on several occasions checked the change when out of sight of the seller, and assured me that it was never a farthing short. The Arab's politeness remains unruffled if you walk out and do not buy. In many instances he will invite you to drink tea or coffee, and not unfrequently will insist on making you accept, gratis, a souvenir from his shop. Perhaps, as we were told, their charges are exorbitant, but none of us could see it.

QUITE FAIR?

So one is much inclined to the view that the hard things said against them are often grossly exaggerated. It was the considered opinion of all of us that they are a most courteous and lovable people. We found them exceedingly friendly. Little boys would walk with us any distance, ready to ask and answer any number of questions. One night two of us got lost in a dark street and an Arab man went far out of his way to put us right. They are light-hearted and enter at once into any prank or joke. I saw a man who must be about thirty crouching behind a corner and waiting to spring a surprise appearance of himself on a friend who walked with the aid of two sticks, and who must have been over fifty. They laugh easily and do not seem to allow this world and its worries to weigh too heavily upon them. At night they gather in the hostels and drink moderately and sing pleasantly in chorus till about ten o'clock. Once or twice we peeped in at indignation meetings but as the addresses were all in Arabic we didn't remain.

You can hear the children in the schools, from early morning, drawling out their lessons aloud in tones reminiscent of our National Schools at home. One day I looked through the books a boy was carrying in his satchel and discovered Hall and Knight's Algebra, and, I think, Moran's French Grammar. English is taught in all the schools and they like to display it whenever foreigners are about.

They are hard to convert; some will say impossible. Four hundred years ago the Franciscans were ordered by their Superiors to discontinue the attempt, as their efforts were barren of any result and in many cases led to the torturing and slaughter of the Friars. When St. Ignatius made his pilgrimage to Jerusalem his zealous heart could not content itself with this programme so he began again to preach to the Arabs, till the

Franciscans heard all about it, got on his tracks, and very promptly and properly clapped this meddlesome apostle into prison! The place where that prison stood is still pointed out, though its authenticity is very doubtful.

But there are happy exceptions. More sterling Catholics than some of these excellent people we have yet to meet. There was, for example, that mother whose husband died and left her helpless with seven young children. A brother of hers, unmarried and well-off, would not look at her. She struggled on bravely alone, never complaining, and she reared a family that is a credit to the Church and to her training. Meanwhile her brother lost all. She opened her door and took him in and made him welcome. For years she has supported him willingly. The two children still with her occasionally break out in complaints. The brother is eighty-four and very troublesome; better pack him off to a home. And the mother replies: "The day you put him out, remember I leave with him." If Christian charity is Our Lord's test of discipleship, that Catholic Arab woman is His disciple indeed.

TENSION

The streets at night are only dimly lighted, a stray candle or oil lamp flickering here and there. We visited an Arab family at home one evening and were shown the carpets and furniture made by the father and sons, and the beautiful pictures painted by the girls. It was a happy home, one hundred-percent Catholic, and considered itself highly privileged to entertain the priest. Each member of the family came forward with much ceremony to kiss your hand, till you began to feel like the Patriarch himself—each member, that is, except the tiny girl of two who was too scared even to glance from the security of her mother's arms in the direction of these strange visitors. Inevitably the conversation turned on the recent disturbances between Jews and Arabs. Many instances were cited to prove that the Arabs were treated with shocking cruelty and injustice, and later on literature was given us, to read at our leisure, which would confirm the truth of the facts recounted.

Certainly there is tension. Some Arab children spat at us, thinking we were Jews. There was a complete change of attitude the moment they understood their mistake. They at once became friendly and apologetic.

Who is right and who is wrong it is not the concern of these pages to discuss or decide, even if the author were in the position to conduct such discussion. We grew to love this generous-hearted people and to sympathize deeply and sincerely with them in the many trials they have to endure. One of our party, in a little farewell speech on the night before we left for Israel, said we were made to feel absolutely at home in Jordan, and that it was with real regret that we realized the time to leave was upon us. Everyone listening was in entire agreement. We cherish the hope of perhaps one day again meeting some of those people whom we came to regard as very dear friends. If ever any of them turn up in Ireland a *céad mile failthe* is certainly waiting for them there.

3. *A Chosen People*

We had Mass one morning in the open air. The altar was set up in the midst of the ruins of the synagogue at Capharnaum. Somewhere near this sacred spot Our Lord had given the promise of the Blessed Eucharist and told the people that unless they ate His Flesh and drank His Blood they could not have life in them. Here He had often disputed with the Jews, refuting their objections and proving by unanswerable arguments His astonishing claim to be the long-promised Messias. The very stones surrounding us on that memorable morning seemed to cry out aloud that they were there and heard Him making the solemn statement that He was the Son of God, in all things equal to His Father, with Whom He is One in nature.

The celebrant of the Mass was a priest whose ardent apostolic heart is wholly set on the conversion of the Jews. If it thrilled us to assist at his Mass in such a unique setting, think what it must have meant to him, to stand there at that altar linking together Christianity and Jewry. For here is the Christian sacrifice being offered in a Jewish synagogue by a Catholic priest! What did it portend?

REDEMPTION OF ISRAEL

Some ten years ago a very learned Jew, Dr. John Friedman, was received into the Catholic Church. He is now a monk and lives in the monastery at Mount Carmel. After his conversion he wrote a remarkable book entitled *The Redemption of Israel*. Briefly, the thesis of that book is that the influx of Jews into Israel in recent years is a foreshadowing of the conversion of the entire race to the Catholic Church. It is a startling thesis, and there are not wanting well-informed and thoughful men who regard it as wishful thinking. But the author has put forward arguments which may not be thus lightly set aside; at the least they are a challenge and a reproach to our apathy.

Non-Catholic Christians have much to teach us here. The sad admission was made to me: "We Catholics are remiss and indifferent by comparison." In every room of our hotel we found a leather-bound copy of the Bible, placed there by the "Gideons." Should a Catholic priest need a copy or copies, they will be only too glad to supply him with as many as he wishes, and all this is *gratis*. High-minded Protestants have made many sacrifices in the effort to spread Christianity among the Jews. The results are far from encouraging, but these missionaries refuse to be beaten. America has spent lavishly on schools and colleges.

And what of the "Roman" Catholics, who are absolutely convinced that they, and they alone, have the full content of the teaching of Christ, and that the Catholic Church is guided infallibly by God's Holy Spirit in spreading it? It would not be fair to say we have been indifferent, but our zeal is "remiss by comparison." Why should this be? Is it because we think the Jews are impossible to convert? Or because we know Jews personally, even many Jews, and we despise their methods and condemn their lust for power and fear their increasing influence in the place we live? It is high time to recall and put into practice the reiterated teaching of the Sovereign Pontiffs that it is gross injustice to blame the entire race for the crimes, real and proven though they may be, of what constitutes only a fraction of that race.

The celebrant of our Mass at Capharnaum implored us to pray for the Jews and, wherever we are, to prove to them by our conduct that no Catholic is, or can be, anti-Semitic. He quoted the courageous words of Pope Pius XI, spoken at a time when anti-Semitism in Germany was at its height. "Notice," said the Pope, "that (in the Mass) Abraham is called our Patriarch, our ancestor. Anti-Semitism is incompatible with the thought and sublime reality expressed in this text. It is a movement in which we Christians can have no part whatsoever. . . . Anti-Semitism is unacceptable; spiritually we are Semites."

When a delegation of Jews came to Rome to ask an audience with Pope Pius XII, they told him of the gratitude felt by all their people for his defense of them and the aid he gave them in their recent persecution. They were received with the exquisite graciousness which has long been recognized as characteristic of the present Holy Father. He welcomed them, telling them they were coming into the home of their common Father, and begging them to try to understand that Catholicism, so far from being inimical to Jewry, is rather its perfect flowering and logical development.

JESUS, THE MESSIAS?

In the mind of many Jews, Christ and Christianity are synonymous with persecution and violence. However deplorable and wide of the mark this attitude may be in actual fact, it is very intelligible indeed in view of past relations between Jews and Catholics, often highly-placed ecclesiastics. Even Protestant writers, like Jakob Jocz, will admit that "it must be said, to the honour of the Church, that officially it never approved of such action" (he is talking about forced baptisms). At the same time he says that "the Christian record of Jewish wrongs and suffering is the most incriminating testimony against the Church." Furthermore, he writes that "whenever an opportunity for revenge occurred, the Jews were not slow to seize it." *

Father Raphael Simon, convert Jew, tells us of the love he had for his religion, and of his iron resolve that "I . . . would never be converted; I would never betray my religion, no matter how much I was persecuted. In becoming a Catholic I fulfilled this resolution." † For he now recognizes that Jesus Christ is come not to destroy but to fulfill. All through the Old Testament there is abundant evidence of God's loving and intimate relations with His People Israel. Why is there a "sudden gap," he asked himself, in these relations from the period after the death of Christ? And the answer? "The mission of the Jews to

* Jacob Jocz, *The Jewish People and Jesus Christ* (London: Society for Promoting Christian Knowledge, 1949), p. 69.

† M. Raphael Simon, O.C.S.O., *The Glory of Thy People* (New York: The Macmillan Company, 1954), p. 3.

bring forth the Redeemer having been fulfilled, and the Catholic Church, the Church of all the nations, having been established, God has dwelt in the midst of it." *

The same truth is brought out in a recent life of another convert Jew, the founder of the Holy Ghost Fathers. His Jewish name was Jacob, which he changed, on becoming a Catholic, to Francis. He is now known to history as Venerable Father Francis Liebermann, and we are permitted to cherish the hope that one day he may be declared a canonized saint. This new life, entitled *Star of Jacob*, makes fascinating reading. Here is a pertinent excerpt:

> Jacob at last unburdened himself to Samson [his brother, who had become a Catholic some years earlier]. Yes, he could understand how the ancient faith had ceased to hold him; for indeed, for several months now, he himself had been beset by doubts. Those miracles, for instance? Why had a God Who was just and loving performed such world-shaking miracles for those early unworthy Israelites who repeatedly fell into sin and paganism; and yet the same God did not lift a finger today for the suffering and abused, holy Jews all over the world, who adored the One God, and who lived, bereft and forlorn, in right-

* *Ibid.*, p. 101.

eousness? His "Chosen People"! There was no sense to it!

To which Samson replied patiently that it was but another proof that Christ was the true Messiah. For, he explained, now that God had sent His only-begotten Son to earth, bearing the richest of miracles to mankind—the Eucharist, the Sacraments—and now that the Son had laid down His life for the redemption of mankind, there was no longer any need for the Father to work the stupendous miracles of the past for his erring children. They had but to turn to Christ.*

The Catholic cannot entertain the smallest shadow of doubt that this is the answer. He knows that Jesus Christ is the Redeemer for Whose coming this people prayed and longed, and because He has come the "sudden gap" has occurred. A friend of mine told me of his efforts to demonstrate this fact to different Jews of his acquaintance. He quoted their own inspired prophets and showed how everything foretold by them is fulfilled to the letter in Jesus Christ. Many Jews have never opened the New Testament, and my friend found that, in many instances, they were not even mildly interested when he opened

* Helen Walker Homan, *Star of Jacob* (New York: David McKay Co., Inc., 1953), p. 123.

it for them. To us Catholics such an attitude seems frankly inexplicable. If Christ made such stupendous claims, you would think that even natural curiosity would prompt them to learn what He had to say by way of proof.

"Generations of Jews," writes Jacob Jocz in his *The Jewish People and Jesus Christ,*

> have lived and passed into oblivion, and though surrounded by Christianity on every side, have never actually faced the truth about Jesus. Equally little have they known about Christianity itself. To the son of Israel, his Christian neighbour remained a Gentile who believed in three Gods, worshipped the Cross and hated the Jews. A large measure of the guilt for this state of affairs falls upon the Church itself; an equally large measure falls upon the spiritual leaders of Judaism.
>
> Conservative Judaism still refuses even to discuss the case of Jesus. Appeals made by enlightened Jews to reconsider the Jewish attitude towards Jesus of Nazareth immediately raise in these quarters an outcry of indignation. Even critical studies of the Life of Jesus made by Jews seem to be, in the eyes of conservative Judaism, an unpardonable sin. . . . Yet more astounding is the fact that this persistent, uncritical, and almost wholesale rejection of Jesus is by no means characteristic of the Orthodox group alone. The attitude of supreme negation is the general rule

for Jewry at large. Here, as nowhere else, do we meet with the lingering memory of Jewish suffering which, in the Jewish consciousness, is closely associated with the name of Jesus. This is the burden of the Christian guilt.*

NEW TESTAMENT

In his sermon at Capharnaum the priest reminded us that Jesus Christ was a Jew Who lived here in this city surrounded by Jews. His Blessed Mother and her husband St. Joseph were Jews who dwelt over at Nazareth. The first apostles were Jews, and to the Jews they first preached the Gospel. Nazareth is spoken of as Our Lord's "own city" and constant reference is made to the Jews as "His own people." He Himself declared that He was sent to the lost sheep of the house of Israel. When these, His own people, would not have Him, He sat on the brow of the hill overlooking Jerusalem, and, strong man that He was, bent His Head forward and shed bitter tears for their sin and broke out into sorrowful lamentations.

Father Raphael Simon describes the first time he picked up a copy of the Gospels and began to read.

* Pp. 64–65.

Little did he expect such interior illumination. The Gospels became a source of comfort such as he had never before experienced and the faithful reading of them paved the way to his firm conviction that Jesus is the promised Messias. "To me as to every Jew," writes Karl Stern, "the very concept of the divinity of Christ was something utterly alien and incomprehensible. It was incompatible with the spirit of the Old Testament, and a blasphemy. . . . It took me very long, nearly ten years, to accept the divinity of Christ . . ." * Given this background it is easy to understand why Jews regard converts to Christianity as renegades and why they scoff at the idea that any Jew comes into the Catholic Church through *intellectual conviction*. Yet there is abundant evidence that he does. Isn't that challenging statement worth putting to the proof?

TOO LONG ASTRAY

The obvious predilection of Our Lord for the Jewish People, even if there were no other argument, is overwhelming in its forcefulness. No true follower

* Karl Stern, *The Pillar of Fire* (New York: Harcourt, Brace and Company, 1951), pp. 178, 179.

of the Good Shepherd but must be filled with grief that this portion of the flock has strayed away. No Catholic dare think or say that a people so loved by God and by Jesus Christ His Son can be permitted to suffer spiritual shipwreck. We may indeed wax eloquent about the crimes of individual Jews, as Jews may, very fairly, lay serious charges at the door of individual Catholics. But it is gross injustice to tar all of us, Jews or Gentiles, with the same brush.

Like his Master, the true Catholic's heart goes out in love to every son and daughter of God on the face of the earth. But if there is any one particular portion of God's great family with special claims upon his love, it is the children of Abraham whom He chose from the beginning.

4. *Israel Today*

The Mandelbaum Gate is the "border" between Israel and Jordan. We were welcomed by a very courteous Jew who, during our interval of waiting, told us of the newly-formed state of Israel. Later, we were to see for ourselves examples of the industry of the people, which built up cities and transformed vast tracts of desert waste into comfortable livings, all within one man's lifetime. The Jews last year (1954) were making solemn celebration of the fiftieth anniversary of the death of Dr. Theodor Herzl, the founder of modern Zionism. In vision this man saw the growth of Israel and set forth what he saw in the form of a novel. What he foretold has come to pass. On all sides Israel gives signs of material prosperity.

1954

The Jewish population has more than doubled in the state since 1948, the restriction limiting the number of Jews entering Israel having been removed in that year. New Jerusalem and Tel Aviv are large cities which have sprung up in the past fifty years; Haifa has a fine harbor; throughout the country you have artificial irrigation making the desert fertile, while farms and settlements house thousands of the people in comfort.

But there are acute psychological problems. Many of the immigrants have widely-differing backgrounds, having come from different countries and pursued different walks of life. Some integrating "process" must be found by means of which to smooth out these differences. Dr. John Friedman, the monk of Mount Carmel, inclines strongly to the belief that this required "process" is Christianity, and that God's purpose in bringing together so many Jews to Israel is to lead them into the Catholic Church. For Christianity does not contradict Jewry; it completes and complements it.

Jewish history began when Abraham crossed the Euphrates about four thousand years ago. For nearly half that time the Jews have been wanderers on the face of the earth. To this day they have preserved between themselves a bond of union, very close indeed, and always they are ready to help and advise each other whenever possible. A young Jew, recently contemplating the claims of Christ and of the Catholic Church, made contact with converts in countries thousands of miles distant. What much impressed the priest who was instructing him was the remarkable fact that it never entered his mind to think they might not bother about him and his queries. Of course they would reply, for they all "belonged." And they did.

BELLOC ON THE JEWS

In all these centuries the Jews have remained a class apart. "Nation after nation," wrote Belloc,

> has absorbed larger, intensely hostile minorities—the Irish, their successive invaders; the British, the pirates of the fifth and eighth centuries and the French of three centuries more; the northern Gauls, their auxiliaries; the Italians, the Lombards; the Greeks, the Slav; the Dacian has absorbed even the Mongol. But the Jew has remained intact.

Why? Is it altogether fantastic to recognize here a special Providence watching over this people and preserving them thus for a special purpose and mission? And, if today many of them no longer consider themselves God's Chosen People, Dr. Friedman would argue that this change does but increase the chance of their becoming Christian. For, as long as they were wedded to their own traditional beliefs, they refused, as we saw, even to consider the case for

Christianity. He brings forward telling evidence to prove that many are now looking toward the Church with a much more tolerant and understanding approach, trusting that perhaps, after all, they may indeed find here the light of truth, lost, as it would seem, with the collapse of what they hitherto believed.

One result of our pilgrimage was to impress upon us the urgency and the need of the apostolate to the Jews. That is partly the reason why we are devoting these pages to them. A missionary in Israel was emphatic that the time is ripe for Catholics to make a serious beginning. He is not foolish enough to expect spectacular or immediate results. There will probably not be much, for a generation or two at least, in the way of visible fruit. "But a start must be made, and right now."

And how? Well, first of all, Catholics everywhere must be roused to an intelligent interest and awareness of this mighty apostolate. A hundred years ago two Jews, the brothers Ratisbonne, were brought into the Catholic Church by means that must seem miraculous. They founded the Order of Sion for the conversion of Israel. Their whole history makes fascinating reading. It has given much impetus to this apostolate, providing as it does abundant evidence of Our Lady's special anxiety for the conversion of her people.

Admittedly, when you look out at four hundred and fifty thousand Jews in Tel Aviv, all absorbed in pleasure and materialism, you are inclined to think there is nothing farther from their minds than any notion of embracing Christianity. And you are quite right. The impression gains according as you contact the people in the farms and settlements and in the other cities of Israel. You say they are of the earth, earthly. And once more your judgment is quite correct. So what? Fold your arms and leave them alone? They do not know what we have to give them. They resent even the suggestion that Jewry has anything to learn from Christianity and stoutly maintain that the shoe is on the other foot. Can we be conscious of our treasure and not try to share it with them? Can we bask contentedly in the sunshine of divine truth and leave them in ignorance of what we are certain to be divine revelation?

WAYS AND MEANS

Thoughts like these quicken the zeal of the Holy Father when he reminds us of the obligation we have to spread the Gospel and tells us it is a "subject of inexhaustible meditation" that other souls depend on us for their eternal salvation. Where would Christianity be if Peter and the first apostles had adopted a defeatist policy when faced with the materialism and gross immorality of Greece and Rome? Here is a field, and we Catholics need to be alert to till it by our prayers, and perhaps even more by our sacrifices. "This kind can be cast out only by prayer and fasting" (Matt. 17:20).

The unity of the Jews among themselves and their undoubted spirit of sacrifice could, under God's grace, be turned to account to form Catholics of sterling worth and indomitable character. If we incline to carp at their secretiveness and tyranny, we have to remember that their history extenuates, even though it cannot always excuse, their faults. The strong wall of prejudice, which has been centuries in building, will take patience and time to batter down. And the battering-ram must be the consistent practice, on the part of us Catholics, of supernatural charity. "By this will all men know that you are my disciples, if you have love for one another" (John 13:35). Here especially must the seed be sown deep in the soil of Israel, to bring forth abundant fruit long after the sower has passed by. Such supernatural love is the sword of the spirit by which to slay the hatred and distrust developed in the Jewish mind by the sad mistakes of Christians in the past. "Why are Jews persecuted?" a prominent Jew was once asked, and he answered: "Because there are too few Christians in the world!"

"But, Father," somebody asked our priest, "you won't fall out with us if we pray also for the conversion of the Arabs, will you?"

The good priest's eyes opened wide in undisguised astonishment. "Of course, pray for the Arabs. If I were sent over to Jordan in the morning I'd work for the Arabs with the same zeal I now employ on behalf of the Jews. And the first step I'd take would be to learn Arabic. It is an immense point in my favor that I can talk to the Jews in Hebrew. Every Jew speaks it here."

Scattered up and down through Israel are tiny groups of Catholics. They assemble every few months for a spiritual retreat and discussion of their problems. If their zeal burns brightly it may well be the spark which later will become a great flame.

"But, Father, can you forget that the Jews crucified Our Lord?"

"But did they? Certainly a section of them was responsible for that crime, but only a section and a small section too. I cannot agree with the view taken by some Catholics that all their sufferings for the past two thousand years are meant to expiate that sin. To me it seems utterly unfair to blame the Jewish nation for the Crucifixion."

5. *Despised Nazareth*

The last few chapters were an effort to supply background. Now that we have at least a rough idea of the "lay-out" of the Holy Land and its people today, we can proceed to visit those hallowed places whose very names are vibrant with memories of the Saviour.

"Can anything good come out of Nazareth?" asked Nathanael in disdain; and he was told to come and see (John 1:46). On November 11, 1954, a bus brought thirty-eight Irish pilgrims to Nazareth that they too might come and see. We drove in by the road leading up from the south, straining our eyes for the first glimpse of the village that cradled Christianity. On sighting it over there to our left on the hillside about four miles off, our hands, as if instinctively, sought our beads. We commenced, as if by common consent, to say the prayer by which Mary has ever been honored in Ireland—the Rosary, followed by the Litany, and the Angelus, which was singularly appropriate. Then began a hymn to our Lady, and the last *Ave* was dying away just as our bus came to a standstill in front of Nazareth's only hotel.

AVE, MARIA!

There was all the business of getting out of the bus and sorting rooms and looking after luggage and taking lunch—an encroachment, you felt, to be dispatched speedily and leave us free to do the things that really mattered and had brought us here. Modern Nazareth is considerably larger than Mary's Nazareth and is situated much lower down. It has about twenty-two thousand inhabitants; roughly one-third are Catholics, Orthodox, and Moslems respectively. There are ten excellent Catholic schools, and the Franciscan Fathers, here as throughout Palestine, are entrusted with the spiritual care of the people. Although Nazareth is in Israel, the vast majority of the people are Arabs.

You are looking for the Church of the Annunciation? Of course you are; every minute seems wasted until you get there. All right. Come out of the hotel and turn left up the broad main street of the town, walking in brilliant sunshine along the sandy surface for seven or eight minutes. Now turn again to your left and climb the rising ground for about ten minutes more. There it is now—the church which has been described, I fear a little extravagantly, as the most beautiful in all Palestine. You assemble for a few minutes in the church grounds and instructions and explanations begin. I'm sure these are well worth listening to, but you strain at the leash. How could you delay when you were aware of the one gigantic truth that loomed so large and alone seemed to matter at this moment—"*Verbum caro hic factum est*"; "*Here* is the place where the Word was made flesh."

Other pens must describe the beauty of the altars and carvings and paintings inside; other pages will be filled with well-deserved tributes to the sons of St. Francis for the monument they have raised here to honor the Mother of God and the Word Incarnate; elsewhere you will read that, in the Marian Year (1954), the foundation stone was laid for a new basilica twice the size of the present church. All this is interesting and edifying. But the pilgrim passing in by that church door has no eyes for all the glory contained within the circumference, preoccupied as he is by the eager, impatient urge to explore the treasure hidden at the center.

Once inside the door, look here to your left—an elevated altar with a flight of steps on each side. Underneath this altar there is a crypt to which you gain access by eighteen or twenty steps of white marble. Go down and at the end draw a long breath. Down here in this crypt there is another altar marking the exact spot where the Word was made flesh and dwelt among us.

CHRISTIANITY AT ITS SOURCE

The Blessed Virgin knelt here, very possibly in this very spot where you have chosen to kneel. This tiny room was one day flooded with heavenly light, for an angel of the Lord entered in to deliver the most stupendous message ever spoken or heard. Where exactly did he stand, and where did Mary kneel? I saw a woman come in here to pray and, when finished, venerate every square inch of that ground. She touched it with her rosary and with her hands, and kissed it over and over again. She could not have failed to contact the sacred spot hallowed by God's angel and God's Mother. She didn't take any risk.

We read St. Luke's account aloud and once more listened to the sublime dialogue. "And when the angel had come to her, he said, 'Hail, full of grace, the Lord is with thee. Blessed art thou among women. . . . Do not be afraid, Mary, for thou hast found grace with God. Behold, thou shalt conceive in thy womb and shalt bring forth a son; and thou shalt call his name Jesus.' " But Mary "was troubled at his word, and kept pondering what manner of greeting this might be." Moreover, there was a difficulty. She has vowed to remain a virgin, so " 'how shall this happen, since I do not know man?' And the angel answered and said to her, 'The Holy Spirit shall come upon thee and the power of the Most High shall overshadow thee; and therefore the Holy One to be born shall be called the Son of God. . . .' But Mary said, '. . . Be it done to me according to thy word ——' " (1:28, 30; 29; 34–36; 38).

Any syllable we might dare to add to the inspired account must seem an unwarranted intrusion, a desecration marring the exquisite simplicity. Can't you see Mary still kneeling here after the angel was gone, her hands crossed over her breast, her eyes closed, her body motionless and slightly bent forward in adoration, everything obliterated from her mind except the one shattering truth that she had become a living tabernacle to house the sacred humanity and divinity of the Son of God?

"*Fiat mihi!*" she had said. "Be it done to me according to thy word!" That "*fiat*" was the maiden's summons to the Second Person of the Blessed Trinity. He would not force Mary to be His mother, for even where there is a question of conferring high honor upon her, He still respects Mary's free will. But on hearing her "*fiat*" the "Omnipotent Word leaps down from Heaven, from His highest throne," and takes flesh of this lowly virgin. "God so loved the world that he gave his only-begotten Son" (John 3:16).

"*Fiat mihi!*" It had all happened here and here it would happen again. For we were back in the early morning, and the summons was repeated by the lips of the priest at Mass and once more "the mystery of divine condescension" was re-enacted before our eyes. "*Ut nobis corpus et sanguis fiat. . . .*" "Let this bread and wine be made the Body and Blood of Christ, for our sakes." This is transubstantiation, the Eucharistic reduplication of the Incarnation, the Word mystically becoming flesh and dwelling with us.

"But when the fullness of time came, God sent his Son" (Gal. 4:4). He sent Him that through Him we might have life and have it more abundantly. This sacred spot is the source of that eternal fountain. Whoever drinks here receives the gift of a new life, the life of sanctifying grace in his soul, by which he shares in a real way in the very life of God Himself. The Incarnation opened that fountain here, in this place where we are kneeling. It is the Catholic's privilege, and his duty, to drink freely himself, and to guide to this source as many as possible of those souls who are thirsting, and whose thirst only God can assuage.

6. *Hill Country*

If Our Blessed Lady had been selfish, she would have stayed on at Nazareth after the Incarnation. Naturally it would have been very much more pleasant to remain here, all alone with her tremendous secret, enjoying the delights of contemplation, rather than undertake a long and perilous journey across the Judean Hills. It was about eighty miles to the house of her cousin Elizabeth, down near Jerusalem, at Ain Karem.

But she went, and went "with haste," partly because she had learned from Gabriel that her kinswoman was also with child and she surmised that she could be of service to her; partly too, I suppose, because she longed to speak of the marvels effected by God in her soul to some one who could appreciate them and discuss them understandingly. Happy indeed is the loving soul who finds in the school of divine love a kindred spirit with similar experiences to its own! The two of them are at once at home with each other; they recognize each other unerringly.

"When God takes possession of a soul," wrote St. John of the Cross, "He does not long remain inactive." So, under the goad of divine love, Mary sped forth into the mountain country, and it was our privilege to accompany her in spirit. The road she took is unknown. A church and a shrine at Ain Karem, about five miles northwest of Jerusalem, have been raised over the traditional spot where the two women met and embraced. You can almost see Elizabeth open the door, shade her eyes for a moment from the glaring rays of the sun, emerge into that open space there in front, look up in Mary's direction, and then break into a smile of welcome as soon as she recognized who her visitor was. Mary had called her from without, and at the sound of her voice the infant in the womb of Elizabeth leapt for joy. "Blessed art thou among women, and blessed is the fruit of thy womb!" (Luke 1:42).

And Mary, in long white flowing gown and veil, standing here in this spot in the midst of these cypress trees, where we too were privileged to stand beside her, stretches out both arms and raises her eyes and head toward heaven, and there, bathed in sunlight, opens her lips and lifts up her heart and proceeds to pour out on the calm evening air the sweet strains of her *Magnificat*. "My soul magnifies the Lord, and my spirit rejoices in God my Savior; because he has regarded the lowliness of his handmaid; for, behold, henceforth all generations shall call me blessed . . . he who is mighty has done great things for me, and holy is his name" (Luke 1:46–49).

ALL GENERATIONS

On that day Mary sounded for the first time the notes of a chord that for twenty centuries has sent forth an echo even to the farthest parts of the earth. As priests we had recited her *Magnificat* every evening at Vespers; as members of her Sodality or Legion we had prayed it in union with her. The Visitation is well named a feast of joy. There was the light of joy spreading itself over the wrinkled face of the old woman who had miraculously conceived the Baptist. Her child in the womb, as she herself had just testified, leapt for excess of joy on this glad occasion. And Mary's expression is a reflection of the heavenly happiness that at this moment is inundating her soul. *Magnificat*—the feast of joy. And we too, Irish pilgrims, tasted it in our own souls; for did we ever dream, in our wildest and fondest dreams, that we would stand here and see and listen to such things?

The Copts and Orthodox vie with us Catholics in

veneration and love for Mary. A young Arab told me about a conversation he had with an Anglican clergyman who had settled down in Jerusalem in order to preach the Gospel there. "You are wasting your time," he told the clergyman bluntly. "In this land all Christians, whatever other lamentable differences they may have, are all united in their attitude toward God's Mother. All of us know how He honored her and elevated her; we remember her inspired prophecy that all generations will call her blessed. We know, furthermore, that the Church you represent does not share these views. You think the honor we show her is derogatory to what is due her divine Son. We've heard it all before, and take it from me, nobody is going to listen to you trying to tell us again."

We went in to visit the church and shrine which tower on the hillside above a grove of cypress trees. A ruin contained here is said to be a portion of the original house. There are paintings illustrating the glorification of Mary through the ages: Duns Scotus, I remember, defending the Immaculate Conception before the Sorbonne, and a picture of the Council of Ephesus in which Mary, to the joy of the entire Catholic world, was declared to be not the Mother of

Jesus the Man only, but in very truth the Mother of God.

One scene showed a group of saints down the years, who were conspicuous for their devotion to Our Blessed Lady. I picked out St. Bernard, St. Teresa of Avila, and a few others. "And not a Jesuit among the whole lot!" "True, Father," grinned the little Friar who was showing us around, "but look again and you'll not find a Franciscan either." This was all very well until we came to the next fresco, right above the High Altar, and beheld St. Francis in glory, flanked on both sides by a whole galaxy of his sons, all fittingly secured in the place of honor, and admittedly nobody is more worthy of it.

THE PRECURSOR

We knelt and prayed and sang together hymns and prayers expressive of the joy that was ours in partaking of this feast of joy. The meeting of the two mothers in this place reminded us to pray especially for good Catholic mothers who would train their children along the lines traced out by Mary and Elizabeth.

After half an hour in Ain Karem we went down the hill directly in front of us and continued along the road to the right for about two miles. A second turn to the right and one soon after to the left and we were standing before the Church of St. John the Baptist, the site of the house where Christ's Precursor was born. Zachary, his father, had built his home up against the eastern side of the mountain, with a cave behind, similar to the cave we were soon to see at Bethlehem. It was a cool retreat in summer, this house, and tradition says that it was here, and in this cave, in a grotto under the nave of the present church, that the saint was born. The cave is hewn out of the solid rock and lighted inside by the lamps always burning there. The ceiling is covered with five bas-reliefs representing some of the events in the life of the Baptist. A stone is pointed out, behind which, it is said, Elizabeth hid her child from the emissaries of Herod.

After John was born, friends and neighbors gathered to offer their congratulations, and the question of giving the baby a name was brought up. Elizabeth wanted him called "John" but the visitors objected that there was no John among the child's ancestors. What would Zachary, his father, think? But Zachary, poor man, had been struck dumb while serving in the temple. An angel had appeared to him to tell him that his wife would bear him a child, though she was now far advanced in years. Zachary refused to believe and as a sign was deprived of the use of speech. So, when now the question of the child's name was put to him, he wrote on a tablet: "John is his name." At once his tongue was loosened and he broke out into a canticle of praise and thanks: "Blessed be the Lord, the God of Israel, because he has visited and wrought redemption for his people . . . as he promised through the mouth of his holy ones, the prophets from old . . . the oath that he swore to Abraham our Father . . ." (Luke 1:68, 70, 73).

This accumulation of wonders set men thinking and questioning. What is going to be the work and mission of this new-born child, seeing that God has surrounded his coming with all these marvels? They had the answer years later, when this same John preached Christ to them at the banks of the Jordan. "Repent," he warned them, "for the kingdom of heaven is at hand" (Matt. 3:2). He was the first of Christian missionaries to Israel. We begged him to bless those into whose hands had passed the apostolate so dear to his heart. A dozen missionaries, thoroughly imbued with his spirit, would swiftly change the face of this land. "Pray therefore the Lord of the harvest to send forth laborers into his harvest" (Matt. 9:38).

7. *Over to Bethlehem*

The journey from Jerusalem to Bethlehem, as we had to make it, is ten miles. The route taken by Our Lady and St. Joseph was only half that distance. But it lay through Israel and was closed to us. Our guide pointed out a portion of it as we drove along. Our bus veered down toward Gethsemani and then southwards, to our right, through the Valley of Cedron. Everywhere the Valley is covered with large flat stones, and each stone marks a burial place. The district has become one huge cemetery, for Arabs and Jews both believe that here will be the scene of the General Judgment, and all, it would seem, are anxious to book early!

By our Irish standards the morning was sweltering—and this was mid-November and letters had described the cold and incessant rains at home. No sign of anything like that here, and you began to recall our Christmas hymn and the mention of the "winter snow" on the night when the Saviour was born. Was there snow, really, in Bethlehem, or were we projecting our own ideas of what ought to be? We were told that, yes, quite probably there was snow. This warm weather was due to break any day now, and then would come three months of torrential downpour, accompanied, very possibly, by bitter piercing winds and snow. The ground, during nine months of un-broken dry weather, has grown too hard to absorb the rains which fall in such force and quantities; so large cisterns have been built and wells sunk, in order to collect and preserve the precious water which must supply the people's needs for another nine months.

If only we could have effected an amicable ex-change—Palestine to give us some of this glorious sun-shine, and we to devise a means of refilling those wells and cisterns at regular intervals!

GOSPEL SCENES

The Gospel becomes alive frequently in this land. That morning, on our way to Bethlehem, we saw shepherds and their flocks. Our Lord speaks about the shepherd leading his flock and compares Himself to a Good Shepherd Whom the sheep follow because they know Him and He calls them by name. Here it is all moving before our eyes. Still do the sheep follow the shepherd and he calls them by name. We had another reminder of the General Judgment also, as in many instances there were goats as well as sheep being guided by the same shepherd. But the goats kept apart. Our Lord explains that at the end He will go forth and separate the good from the bad, just as a shepherd separates the sheep from the goats. Somebody remarked that the black shaggy goats, with horns twisted everywhere, were exceedingly ugly and might well represent the lost souls. Fair enough, though it must be admitted that the poor sheep were not much to admire either.

Camels too we passed along the way, here and elsewhere. They proceed at a very dignified pace, supercilious to a degree, aloof, and with disdain written on their faces as they deign barely to glance over in our direction. There are eight names for God, we were told, which are known to the Arabs. There is a ninth name, but it only the camel knows. Hence his air of superiority! One of my friends thinks that what we heard is that there are ninety-nine names known to the Arab, and the hundredth is known to the camel. He probably has the tale correct. But anyhow the point is clear.

Pleasantries and interests like these were all right in their way, but we were only mildly responsive. The thought uppermost in the minds of all of us was, that like the shepherds of those hills two thousand years ago, we too were going over to Bethlehem. Our guide indicated Shepherds' Hill, about two miles south of the town, where they were minding their flocks on that cold night, when presently the sky—that sky, up there—was flooded with light and the silence was broken by the wondrous message and song of the angels. Poor illiterates, but He thought it worthwhile to summon them to His court, and in this manner summon them, preferring their simplicity and sincerity to the pride and ceremonial and hypocrisy of the palaces of kings.

AUDIENCE CHAMBER

"Let us go over to Bethlehem and see this thing that has come to pass, which the Lord has made known to us" (Luke 2:15). That is exactly what we ourselves were doing now, preparing to have an audience in the King's Court, believing, as the shepherds believed, with childlike faith, that the Infant we were going to find wrapped in swaddling clothes and laid in a manger, is, in very truth, the Son of God, one with and in all things equal to His Eternal Father.

It is fitting that subjects arrive first and stand till the King enters, but at Bethlehem the King was already in waiting. "Jesus Christ, yesterday, today, and the same forever" can dispense with conventions, and, in the fascinatingly attractive form of a tiny baby lying in the lap of a beautiful young mother, He gives audience to this group of Irish pilgrims, welcoming them and making them feel quite at home, as shepherds and Magi surely felt at home when they found Him here.

We climbed down into the crypt on the Epistle side of the Franciscan Church and found ourselves at the mouth of the cave. Here to our left is the spot where He was born; we each knelt in turn on both knees to venerate it. Then, a few paces to the right you have the altar of the manger, where His mother placed Him and protected Him as best she might from the icy winds. In the dim light each of us priests stood there and celebrated Mass, placing Him there again to be adored by our people, giving Him into their loving embrace in Holy Communion, as Mary, no doubt, might have entrusted Him for a while into the arms of shepherds and Magi.

The cave is small and the rock hard to keep kneeling upon, and the many oil lamps and candles burning made the air heavy and oppressive. But our faithful people remained for one Mass after another—breakfast could wait, or if necessary be dispensed with, but never again would they have a chance like this. A unique opportunity not to let slip at any cost.

St. Ignatius Loyola, the erstwhile soldier who later became as a little child, bids me "to see Our Lady and St. Joseph and the serving-maid; also the Infant Jesus after His birth, accounting myself a poor and unworthy servant, looking at and contemplating them and tending them in their necessities as though I were present there, with all possible homage and reverence; and after that to reflect on myself in order to derive some profit."

"As though I were present there." But the thought that must ever burn like a bright light in the pilgrim's mind is that he was there. He saw and he heard, and, as also happened in the case of the shepherds, he wants to tell everyone. For if the whole world was to crowd into this little cave, room would somehow be found. Even as He lies in His mother's arms the Child seems today to speak that invitation: "Come to me, all you who labor . . . I will give you rest" (Matt. 11:28).

The birth happened here because there was no room at the inn. Jesus, Mary, and Joseph have experience of all their plans being upset and of losing their little home up at Nazareth. They are displaced persons, homeless wanderers, and their example of fortitude is a staff upon which many lean for support today. Nor does the staff bend or break, despite the pressure.

AROUND THE TOWN

We were able to have several hours in and about Bethlehem. We wanted to meet the people and try to experience for ourselves what the atmosphere was like; so we wandered here and there and engaged in conversation wherever we could. The town is more than two thousand feet above sea level, built on two hills, the higher one of which was the site of the place where Jesus was born. The streets, like the streets in Jerusalem, are rather narrow and somewhat gloomy, but the gloom is dispelled by the cheery smile that greets you from the Arabs everywhere. There was also, and inevitably, the effort to induce the simple stranger to buy. One of our party purchased a crib, such a gem as to deserve special mention, each figure exquisitely carved. It is a present for some lucky little boy in England.

We found our way into an Armenian church. The priest bade us welcome and showed us the altar and vestments, and read an extract aloud for us from the missal. We asked him kindly to translate, and what was our surprise to hear him speak the words: "Thou art Peter, and upon this rock I will build my Church and the gates of hell shall not prevail against it" (Matt. 16:18). Here was coincidence! We ventured to tell him what we believe that the Pope is Peter's successor, and that the Church founded on Peter is the Catholic Church. He smiled tolerantly and a friendly discussion ensued. But we did not convert him, nor he us!

It was the hour of the school "break" and children were swarming all over the place. They laughed and shouted and pulled each other about and ran after each other to play something like "tag." Some fortunate ones had secured a precious coin or two and they made for the sweet shop. We saw them jostling each other excitedly as they stood by the counter, pointing with index finger to the jar of sweets of their choice, eyes popping as they watched the woman of the shop counting out the right number, and presently returning to their friends in the street to share or to bargain for an exchange. Small boys are the same the world over, it would seem—in Bethlehem as in Ballyfermot!

The thought of that "winter snow" kept coming back to my mind. It seems to have some special significance. Remembering there are nine months of glorious sunshine, why does God's divine Son choose by preference the one brief spell of cold weather? Isn't the choice like that of the period of exceptional difficulty selected for the Passion—when Jerusalem was crowded? He seems to go out of His way, not only to do what is hard, but to do the hard thing in circumstances which add to the sacrifice it already calls for. But love is like that, and only love can explain the Incarnation and all that follows. And the true lover is well aware that love rings truest on the anvil of suffering endured for the sake of those who are loved.

8. *Back to Nazareth*

Our Lord spent nearly the whole of His life at Nazareth. So it will well repay a second visit. In another chapter we went in spirit into the Church of the Annunciation and prayed together in the room where the angel of the Lord declared unto Mary. Today we come out of that church and, on once more reaching the grounds outside, we turn to the right and walk for just three or four minutes till we come to the house of St. Joseph. After Our Lady was betrothed to Joseph, she left her own house and lived here, and, after the return from Egypt, it was here too that the Holy Family settled till Christ went out on His public missions.

The Franciscans have built a church on the site of Joseph's workshop. The home of the Holy Family, like many other homes even to this day, was set up in the vicinity of a cave in the rock. This cave served as an extra bedroom, or as a shelter for cattle, or as a storeroom or workshop. It is most likely that it was here that Joseph plied his trade, using saw and plane and hammer and nails, earning what was needed to keep the roof over their heads. Here, too, the Son of

God would have stood beside him, learning how to become a good tradesman and gratefully receiving directions from His foster father. Of course He knew all about it already; of course He could employ methods far superior to any He could learn from poor Joseph. But He stands there in His bare feet, in the midst of shavings and sawdust, and listens and obeys, exactly as He is told. God Himself willing to be taught—a rebuke to those of us who cannot suffer a word of advice or correction, how tactfully soever it be spoken.

WHAT NAZARETH IS LIKE

I had always envisaged Nazareth as tucked away in a sort of pocket in the hills. I fancied that if, in Mary's time, you could have gone up in a plane and looked down, what you would have seen would be a large capital "Y," one long street branching out, as it climbs the hill, into two narrow streets. It was gratifying to be assured, on the actual spot, that all this is correct. So I placed the home of the Holy Family at the extreme of the right-hand arm of the "Y."

On the extreme of the left-hand arm stood, and still stands, the synagogue. At the junction of the three roads you have the Fountain of Mary, the only well in Nazareth today and for centuries. Almost a mile from the synagogue is the Hill of Precipitation, concerning which we shall have to say a word presently. All this should give a fairly definite picture: the whole town like a "Y," with the two Churches of the Annunciation and of the Holy Family on the end of the right arm, the Fountain of Mary at the junction of the three roads, and the synagogue and Hill of Precipitation on the left-hand arm.

There seems to be no doubt that Our Lady came to this well to draw water. Very probably she brought Jesus in her arms with her as long as He was a baby, and later He would have toddled along by her side holding His mother's hand. Later still and He would have visited the well alone, for he is now a boy, doing His share of the household chores, one of which would be to get the water and bring it back. An apocryphal gospel relates that it was here at this well that the Incarnation took place, the voice of the angel addressing Mary as she filled her pitcher and prepared to return with it to the house.

While we were looking on, a girl came on the scene with pitcher balanced on her head. She opened the gate of the well, walked over to the spring, removed the pitcher and filled it, and with practiced hand swiftly and securely replaced it on her head. She walked away, with dignified stride, in the direction of the town. We noticed this dignity of poise in all the women out here, cultivated by the rigidity and balance they must develop in order to carry things steadily on their heads.

As we kept watching her, once more the Gospel became alive. This girl might have been Mary of Nazareth—the Mother of God was thus simple, thus unassuming, her exterior life in no way differing from that of any other girl or woman in the village. All the beauty was within, in her soul where she treasured the King's secret.

"SUBJECT TO THEM"

Some people think that Our Lord did not attend school. They remind us of the question later put by His townsfolk: "How does this man come by learning, since he has not studied?" (John 7:15). But all this question implies is that He had no higher education, as a scribe in the rabbinical school. This is consistent with the supposition that He went to school like other boys. He was like us in everything except sin;

would He be likely to make Himself singular by staying at home when the whole village was at school?

So if you will please stay on here at this well for another few minutes and look back over the road you have travelled, up along the right-hand arm of the "Y," you can get a view of the house of Joseph. It is early morning, about seven o'clock, and you see the door of the kitchen open out onto the street. The mother has had to open it, for the latch is still too high for Him to reach. Perhaps God's mother kissed or embraced her Son as, with His writing slate clutched under His right arm, holding books and the lunch she would have prepared, He came out and joined some companions and walked with them down toward the spot where the three roads converge. Arrived there, they would have turned and climbed up the left-hand arm of the "Y" until they reached the synagogue, where classes corresponding to our National School in Ireland were usually held. The rabbi was there, counterpart of our teacher at home. The boys filed in, there was a short prayer, all seated themselves, books were opened, and the day's tasks began. All we know from the Gospel about this period of Our Lord's life—except for the story of the Finding in the Temple—is comprised in a single sentence:

"He . . . was subject to them" (Luke 2:51). He obeyed the minister of the synagogue as He obeyed Mary and Joseph; He obeyed, as later still He would be subject to Annas and Caiphas and Pilate, for all authority is from God.

There is one memorable occasion when He came to the synagague. We stood there together and opened St. Luke at the fourth chapter and saw the whole drama once more unfold itself before our eyes. "And Jesus returned in the power of the spirit into Galilee; and the fame of him went out through the whole country. And he taught in their synagogues, and was honored by all. And he came to Nazareth, where he had been brought up; and according to his custom, he entered the synagogue on the Sabbath and stood up to read. And the volume of Isaias the prophet was handed to him. And after he opened the volume, he found the place where it was written, 'The Spirit of the Lord is upon me; because he has anointed me; To bring good news to the poor he has sent me, to proclaim to the captives release . . .' And closing the volume, he gave it back to the attendant and sat down. And the eyes of all in the synagogue were gazing on him. And he began to say to them, 'Today this Scripture has been fulfilled in your hearing.' And all

bore him witness, and marvelled at the words of grace
that came from his mouth" (Luke 4:14–22).

REJECTION

But presently the fickle wind of popular favor veers
in another direction. An attitude of hostility has been
created, for this fearless man does not hesitate to up-
braid His hearers for the crime of rejecting Himself.
"And all in the synagogue, as they heard these things,
were filled with wrath. And they rose up and put him
forth out of the town, and led him to the brow of a
hill . . . that they might throw him down headlong.
But he, passing through their midst, went his way"
(Luke 4:28–30).

The place is called the Hill of Precipitation. Close
by stands the Chapel of the Fear of Mary commemo-
rating the terror that surely must have seized upon
the heart of His mother that day, when she thought
the infuriated mob would have its way.

"Can anything good come out of Nazareth?"
(John 1:46). "Search the Scriptures and see that out
of Galilee arises no prophet" (John 7:52). As we con-
tinue to ponder in our hearts, like Mary, on all we see
and hear in this hallowed spot, the immensely com-
forting and sustaining truth deepens in the mind that

the garment of sanctity is woven from very common material indeed. Our own lives are so drab. We have been disillusioned about so many things: ideals which appealed once have come crashing down about our ears; people we trusted have been proven traitors; schemes upon which we embarked with zest have petered out; our daily lives are so ordinary, so lacking in opportunity. For a thousand such reasons we find ourselves giving up the effort to become holy.

But could any life be more drab than in this little village of Nazareth where everyone knew everyone else's business, and was not slow to poke his nose into it if it happened that he was uninformed? What opportunity did this backwater place afford for achievement, for winning the world to Himself? But here He remained just the same, when the whole world needed Him sorely and was crying out for Him. Here He passed thirty long years, well aware that His allotted span was only thirty-three. Here He allowed time to be wasted. When He could have been swaying whole multitudes by His divine eloquence and miraculous powers, He merely stands learning the trade at Joseph's carpenter's bench, He merely goes up to the school in the synagogue, or takes the pail, at Mary's bidding, to fetch the water for their evening meal. It doesn't add up, somehow.

STANDARDS

"For my thoughts are not your thoughts; nor your ways my ways, saith the Lord. For as the heavens are exalted above the earth, so are my ways exalted above your ways, and my thoughts above your thoughts" (Isai. 55:8–9). It is well to stay down here, in despised Nazareth, far removed from the tumult of the modern world, away from its rivalries and ambitions, forgetting its record-breaking exploits, deaf to the roar of its traffic, blacking out the make-believe of its cinema and television. It is good to visit Nazareth often to check up on one's standards of value. The world we live in, the world which claims us or tries to claim us and possess us soul and body, looks very different when seen through the eyes of the Son of God.

If you look through binoculars at a small object, they will make it seem very big. But if you use your binoculars wrong way round, objects that actually are large appear quite small. We use the glasses wrong way round, very generally, when we turn them on to Nazareth, and correctly only when we focus them on the world and its interests. Jesus Christ inverted the process. In this He is the true revolutionist, and His summons is to revolution also.

9. *Night by the Lakeside*

The night by the Sea of Galilee is an unforgettable experience. We were looking forward to it, and friends who had been there had been telling us of its beauty and its atmosphere; and to say we were not disappointed is to utter the last word in understatement. We had driven up from Mount Thabor and reached the ruins of Tiberias about three in the afternoon. Some dismounted and decided to remain here and take a dip. Others preferred to stay in the bus and drive around the coast of the Lake for about another seven miles, in the southern direction. Our priest-guide strongly advocated this latter course and I am glad I followed his advice.

For this is the district where Our Lord spent more of His public life than anywhere else. He had walked along that waterfront, had watched the men fishing from their boats on this Lake, had stood by at the shore and looked on while they were mending their nets, or sorting out from the fishes caught those worth keeping and those to be flung back again into the water. And, as He stood there one day, He spoke to some of those fishermen. "Come, follow me," He said, "and I will make you fishers of men" (Matt. 4:19). The invitation seemed irresistible, somehow. What exactly it implied those men could not have entirely explained to you. But they felt no sense of risk. There was some indefinable attractiveness about this man; so forthwith "they left their nets and their father, and followed him" (Matt. 4:22).

But indeed every side was fragrant with memories of Him. We shall return to some of them again.

KIBBUTZ

Our driver, a Jew, was anxious we should visit a *Kibbutz*, one of the many Jewish settlements dotting the countryside. This one, close to the lake, began forty-five years ago with ten Russian Jews. It now numbers five hundred, all of whom form a single community and live a "communal life." They eat at the same table and each section has its allotted portion of work, all between them contributing to the upkeep of the whole. Some run the farm, others repair the buildings, the women do the housework and the cooking and mending—for all and sundry, I think. There are schools on the spot for the children and from their earliest years every care is taken to instill in them a love of the soil. If a child shows any special aptitude, opportunity will be provided for him to develop it.

As we walked around, my mind turned to the thought of the Jesuit "Reductions" in Paraguay. These were settlements too, formed by the Jesuit Fathers for the benefit of the natives, and for a hundred and fifty years priests and people co-operated with the happiest possible results. But there is one enormous difference between the experiment in Paraguay and that in Israel. At Paraguay the first place was given to God. "The Lord thy God thou shalt adore and Him only shalt thou serve." The settlers in the "Reductions," like the early Christians, had all things in common, and like them too, many of them attained to the practice of heroic sanctity. The temptation is strong to digress here and give a detailed account of the work done and the fervor maintained and the constancy preserved of those Christians in Paraguay. But that digression would take us too far afield.

Of course you will have guessed what the big difference was which we noted as we walked about the *Kibbutz*. There were undoubted signs of material prosperity and the people seemed contented and most industrious. But, somehow, you were not surprised when you were told that God is left out. You sensed that. We experienced nothing but courtesy, but I'm afraid we felt the atmosphere somewhat depressing all the same. All Jews here read the Old Testament, at least as a classic, and, on reaching adult age, each decides for himself on the question of religion. In some of the settlements there are regular religious instructions—in how many I forgot to ask—but in this particular one, none.

THE BLISS OF HEAVEN

I think we were all glad to get back into our bus and return along the coast to Tiberias where we had left our friends. Having collected them we proceeded to the Mount of Beatitudes, on the northwestern side, where we were to spend the night. It was up here that Our Lord, early in His public life, gathered a crowd around Him, and "opening his mouth" preached what has since been known as the Sermon on the Mount. The Franciscan nuns have a hostel here, and on the walls of their octagonal Church, all the way round, you have engravings in Latin of the Eight Beatitudes, one on each wall. We filed into this church that evening and it was the author's great privilege to deliver a "sermon on the mount," in the exact place where the Master had sat and taught the multitudes.

Later we passed out on to the porch and watched a superb moonrise, and then dispersed, singly or in little groups, to pray and meditate or talk quietly as we walked about in the footsteps of Christ Our Lord.

From this elevation you looked across the lake and kept feasting your eyes on that full moon slowly creeping up behind the hills and out into a cloudless blue sky. At your feet was the sea, motionless and silent and without a ripple, smooth as a sheet of glass. "I heard not a sound nor a foot-step, save only God's and my own." Thank heaven men's hands have not spoiled this by building up cities along the coast. Thank heaven they cannot change those hills or those waters. This is the stillness you longed for. In such a perfect setting He had walked up the slope of that hill over there on your left, having dismissed the crowds, and on reaching the summit He had knelt down to pray. "And he continued all night in prayer to God" (Luke 6:12). You could almost see Him, that figure in white, kneeling motionless, with hands clasped tight and with the rays of the moon shining down upon Him. The whole world with its trivialities seemed so senseless up here. Here one seems to touch reality as one contemplates Christ in prayer, His whole being plunged into this sacred act, His Sacred Heart on fire with love of the Father, His anxiety for man's true interests lending zest to the petitions He pours forth for them as He prays in this place.

STORM ON THE LAKE

Down at the shore—can't you see it?—the crowds had dispersed, reluctantly enough; and the apostles, unwillingly too, had put out to sea at His command. I came upon the ruined wall of a little, unused old shack and sat on a rock near it so as to have shelter from the wind. It was a warm wind, quite gentle at first, but I did hope it might gather force and develop into one of those sudden storms which we know can happen here. Actually it didn't. But it was in the midst of such a storm, on a certain night long ago, that a tiny boat was tossed up and down out there on those waters, while the Master, all oblivious as it would seem of the imminent danger threatening His friends, continued to pray on that mountain.

But presently, as you look over, you observe a slight movement in that hitherto motionless figure. He rises from His knees, gathers the folds of His garment together in His right hand, descends swiftly and with firm step along the slope, and without in the least slackening His pace, proceeds to walk on the surface of the waves in the direction of the terrified little party. It was just such a night as this, and they could see Him in the full moon. "It is I," He told them above the roar of the waves. "Do not be afraid." Peter, all impetuous in the eagerness of his love, feels the urge to be wherever Christ is. "If it is thou," he shouts back, "bid me come to thee over the water." And Jesus answers: "Come" (Matt. 14:27, 28, 29).

Out climbs Peter to advance to Our Lord, and sure enough, to his amazement, he finds that he too can walk on the waves. "But seeing the wind was strong, he was afraid and . . . began to sink." Poor Peter, the moment his faith began to falter and to depend on himself, down he went. But Christ was by his side in a moment to rescue him and the entire group. This is where it had happened.

INTO THE DEEP

One day the multitudes flocking around Our Lord were so great that there was danger that they might push Him into the sea in their eagerness to get near and catch what He was saying. This place was then a busy center and afforded the Preacher the opportunity He sought to deliver His message. On this occasion He beckoned to Peter and asked Him for permission to step into his fishing smack. They pulled off a little, and the Master, seated in the boat, spoke to the crowds who stood or squatted there on the land. He would not permit the gracious act of Peter to go without its reward. For, when He had finished speaking, they rowed out into the deep and enclosed a miraculous catch of fishes. It was then that Peter, overpowered by the sudden realization that had come to him, fell down on his knees before Our Lord, exclaiming: "Depart from me, for I am a sinful man, O Lord" (Luke 5:8).

Over there on the other side is the country of the Gerasenes. It was here that He expelled the devil from a man, and the evil one besought Him for leave to enter into the swine. A flock of swine was feeding over there and, as soon as the devil had entered into the animals, they rushed headlong down that incline into the sea.

After the Resurrection He stood here on the shore and watched Peter and John fishing from their boat. They had labored all the night and had caught nothing. But, at His word, they put down the net just once more, and again took a miraculous catch, so big that the nets were breaking.

ETERNAL REST

Then followed that inexpressibly lovely scene, where Peter, his clothes dripping with the water of the lake, knelt in front of Christ and, his rough, weather-beaten hands resting in the hands of his Lord and Master, and his eyes riveted upon Him, made his triple confession. Love Thee, Lord? "Lord, thou knowest all things; thou knowest that I love thee" (John 21:17). And the repentant sinner is forthwith raised up to the loftiest eminence. The first Vicar of Christ on earth is Peter who denied Him, cursing and swearing that he knew not the man. That is how Christ forgives.

Is it fair to see in this event a foreshadowing of the great final examination on the shore of eternity? Like Peter and John we too are out on the chopping sea of this world, feeling perhaps that it is dark night, and that all our efforts have been futile. The examination is ahead of us, and we know exactly on what it is going to turn. "When the evening of life comes," says St. John of the Cross, "you will be judged on love."

It was a natural enough transition of thought, after this, to recall, as one sat there in the shelter of the shack, the procession of those souls whom one had known in life and who had now gone through

Nazareth

Sea of Galilee

that final examination. You felt at home with your dear dead, in this midnight silence, under this azure canopy, with that glowing lamp reflecting its beauty and its glory in those still waters below. Here He had once said to those waves: "Peace, be still" (Mark 4:3). And there followed a great calm. You prayed too for them all: "Eternal rest give to them, O Lord; may they rest in peace!"

SCHOOL OF PRAYER

It was like a monastery up here during the period of the "Great Silence." Not a sound, except the occasional twitter of a cricket. But God was in this silence, to be felt almost palpably. As morning began to dawn you heard the cock crow. But neither did that intrude on the prayerfulness of this sanctuary. It too fitted in perfectly, for surely Peter had often stood and listened to it here, and each time learned anew a message that brought to his eyes tears of sweet repentance. "A contrite and humble heart, O Lord, thou wilt not despise" (Ps. 50:19).

They were all here with us on this wonderful night, to share with us in our vigil the knowledge and the love they had imbibed from contact with Christ.

Nor was it mere fancy that made us see Him too, kneeling over there in prayer. Catholics know He is with them still. All that night the nuns, at our suggestion, had left the Church open, and the sanctuary lamp sent forth its flicker of light to assure us He was in the tabernacle as of old on that hill.

On another occasion they had importuned Him: "Lord, teach us to pray" (Luke 11:1). It seemed easy and natural to pray up here. On every side there were echoes of His voice and evidence of the touch of His hand and signs that His feet had walked this way. No lesson does the divine Teacher more willingly undertake than to direct His disciples in the school of prayer. And no setting could be conceived more conducive to learning than the Sea of Galilee, wrapped about in the stillness of night, and over your head the golden lamp, lighted by God's hand and set up in His heaven. Mary, His mother, is said to be "fair as the moon." Why, you understand better, after a night by the lakeside.

I very much wanted to watch the sunrise break out into its full splendor over the waters. But it was time for Mass now and we went inside. Up above the altar of Beatitudes another sun arose, the Light of the World. He is still at Galilee and Catholics know it.

But not at Galilee only, but wherever there is a tabernacle and the Eucharist. Catholics know that too. Wherever they are, they walk within the circumference of the circle of light cast by the sanctuary lamp.

10. *By Jacob's Well**

A Greek priest was in charge at Jacob's Well. He was middle-aged, wore a tattered, discolored old cassock, was of medium height, with hooked nose and jet-black hair and beard and, perched on his head, the turret-shaped, rimless hat commonly used by them, varying in height from about four to six or seven inches. He gave the impression of being a person who took life exceedingly seriously; he was most grave and reserved in manner; he was sallow of complexion, and across his brow there was a perpetual frown which kept you all the time wondering if he ever was guilty of the indiscretion of breaking into a smile. In tolerably good English he recalled for us the fascinating story of Jesus and the Samaritan woman.

DYNAMITE!

She had come here to draw water. She came alone and in the middle of the day. A reason for this, put forward tentatively, makes both details significant.

* Scripture quotations for this chapter are taken from the fourth chapter of St. John's Gospel. Verse numbers are given in parentheses after each quotation.

80

For it was, and still is, the custom of the women to travel to the well in each other's company, and to wait for each other until all the pitchers are filled. They all chat and laugh and discuss the events of the day. But this poor woman? She is an outcast, a public sinner, and with her no self-respecting citizen would wish to associate.

Little did she suspect how the citadel of sin in her soul was to be dynamited that day. "Jesus, therefore, wearied as he was from the journey, was sitting at the well" (6). Exhausted by the length of the road through Samaria and by the sun beating down mercilessly on His head, He had halted here. The well today is covered by a dwelling-house, but in His time there was probably just a shed over it, under which Our Lord would gladly have sat to escape for a while from the scorching rays. He sat on this ledge which the Greek priest strokes with his hand as he explains.

The woman took no notice at all, for the man was a Jew, and to this very day "Jews do not associate with Samaritans" (9). The Jews worship at Jerusalem, but the Samaritans at Mount Garazim, just outside; we could see it from where we were standing. Four times each year all Samaritans assemble on this mountain for special services. They number, all told, somewhat less than three hundred at the present, because they never intermarry with other peoples. Our Lord explained to the woman that "the hour is coming when neither on this mountain nor in Jerusalem will you adore the Father" (21). The religion of Jesus Christ would spread throughout the whole world; the commission He would give His apostles would be to preach the Gospel to every creature.

It would be beyond the scope of this chapter to give a complete account of the conversation which took place here between Jesus and the woman. He begins by telling her about the meaning and power of sanctifying grace, using the water here to illustrate its effects on the soul. "The water that I will give him shall become in him a fountain of water, springing up unto life everlasting" (14). The poor thing only dimly grasps the meaning of what He is saying, but at least she would be glad to drink such water. "Sir, give me this water that I may not thirst, or come here to draw" (15). How fully He would comply with that request; how readily it has been granted to every soul who, sensing that in Him alone is happiness, seeks in Him to allay its thirst!

"I AM HE"

Next He makes her confession for her. "Jesus said to her, 'Thou hast said well, "I have no husband," for thou hast had five husbands, and he whom thou now hast is not thy husband'" (17–18). Swiftly comes the dramatic climax. "The woman said to him, 'I know that the Messias . . . when he comes . . . will tell us all things.' . . . Jesus said to her, 'I who speak with thee am he'" (25–26).

St. Ignatius worked hard to reclaim women of this class. A wiseacre thought fit to warn him he was only wasting his time. "If I succeed," came the answer, "in keeping one single girl off the streets for one night, even with the certain knowledge that she will go back the next night, I consider all my trouble to be amply repaid." At Sichar that day there was a rich harvest indeed to the sickle of the divine Reaper: for the woman was transformed into an apostle. "I who speak with thee am he." It was another example of the power of grace. She had recognized Him; she knew He was God. Beside that shattering realization every other interest disappeared like mist before the sun. The day a soul recognizes Him for Who He is— recognizes, not merely assents to the truth in the cold regions of the intellect—is a red-letter day in the history of that soul. Life can never again be the same.

Nor was it for the poor sinful woman. She rushed back into the city, leaving her pitcher there at the well in the eagerness of her excitement. She ran up and down the streets stopping everyone to gather them around her and to tell them her astounding news. She had found the Messias! Let them go at once to the well and see for themselves. The whole town turned out. They listened spellbound to what He had to say. They wanted to keep Him with them altogether, Jew though He be. "They besought him to stay there; and he stayed two days" (40).

What were we to dwell upon most as we stood in this sacred place; the mercy of Christ, friend of sinners; the divine condescension bending with such graciousness to this woman despised and scorned by the haughty and self-righteous; the instantaneous change effected in her; or the welcome extended by the hostile Samaritans to this Jewish rabbi?

"GIVE ME TO DRINK"

"Sir," the woman had said, "thou hast nothing to draw with, and the well is deep" (11). The priest told us the depth is one hundred and eighty feet. Were we a little skeptical? Or perhaps he wasn't too strong on numerals in English. He let a pebble drop in and bade us cock our ears to listen and hear it, some seconds later, touch the surface of the water below. The distance is about eighty feet. I shall always regret that I did not drink of the water from the same well from which Our Lord had almost certainly drunk. It did not occur to any of us, somehow, to say, like Him: "Give me to drink," and the priest did not make the suggestion. The windlass is there, just as one sees it in paintings of the scene.

Anyhow, the good priest's attention was by this time somewhat diverted. His explanations, you see, were nearly ended and some of us were beginning to move away. We noticed him glancing apprehensively in the direction of one of the doors, and then, very deliberately, he stopped talking and walked up the few steps leading to the exit. We watched while he dived into the pocket of his cassock, produced a key, and locked the rest of us in! The "baksheesh" was important and he wasn't taking any risks! But indeed we heard that the Orthodox are definitely poor, and none of us begrudged this good man whatever he collected.

The Arabs, friendly as ever, closed in about us

from all sides when we called a halt at the city of Nablus, the ancient Neapolis, birthplace of St. Justin Martyr. We were conducted to a hotel for lunch and afterwards strolled on to the porch to see what was to be seen. What comes back to my memory at this moment is a procession of donkeys we saw, each unfortunate beast heavily laden with a load of clay which the owner, for reasons best known to himself, was transferring from one place to another. Whoever escapes hard work out here, it is not the donkey. We saw longsuffering donkeys being belabored while carrying weighty burdens—water, bricks, stone, bales of cloth, baskets of clay. For any sort of old agglomeration, the natural thing to do with it seems to be to heave it up onto a donkey's back.

PLAY UP!

Some Arab boys, in the street below our porch, were playing a game. Their ball hopped up to where we were standing and when we threw it back to them, an impromptu match began between them and us, to their obvious delight. When, half an hour later, we got into the bus, it seemed as if the whole town had gathered to give us a good send-off. Such smiling, and handshaking, and cheering, and wavings of farewells!

We went to call upon the Samaritan High Priest in his Samaritan synagogue, a rather gaunt and ugly building, with a flight of stone steps outside. As it happened, he was not at home, but we were introduced to his son and to another priest, who was taking his place that day. He showed us the Pentateuch, which he called the oldest book in the world. It consists of the five books of Moses, written on parchment scrolls, and preserved in a silver cylinder. To our amazement he passed it to us and allowed us to handle it and to feel the scrolls. No wonder they show unmistakable signs of rough handling.

The Samaritans do not believe in the divinity of Christ, but this priest reminded us of the anxiety Our Lord showed for the sinful Samaritan woman. He recalled that when Our Lord cured ten lepers He was stung by the ingratitude of the nine who forgot to come back and say their word of thanks, and consoled that at least one remembered, and that a Samaritan. He told us the story of the good Samaritan who helped the man who fell among the robbers, opening his purse to pay for his lodging and food. And he more than insinuated that if any of ourselves opened ours and helped him with funds for a Samaritan Boys'

School he would be assuredly the very last person in the world to breathe a word of objection!

What he conveniently forgot to mention was that "many of the Samaritans of that town [Sichar] believed in him because of the word of the woman who bore witness. . . . And far more believed because of his word" (39, 41). These latter "said to the woman, 'We no longer believe because of what thou hast said, for we have heard for ourselves and we know that this is in truth the Savior of the world' " (42).

We carried away with us photos of the High Priest, bearded and in flowing robes and bearing his signature; beside him the cylinder containing the Pentateuch. When we showed these to our guide he remarked that he knew him very well. The Samaritans are very poor and the High Priest turns up in Jerusalem to seek aid from a Catholic society corresponding to the St. Vincent de Paul. "He'll soon be along now," said our guide, "to tell us about your visit and ask for help." One expects that if he did he fared well, for the society is run by the Franciscan Fathers along lines that are in the best tradition of Franciscan charity.

11. *Jericho*

Why do people tell you go to Jericho? Is it a euphemism for going to hell? When you remember that Jerusalem, only fifteen miles from Jericho, is well over two thousand feet above sea level and Jericho more than eight hundred feet below, you are not surprised that the mind easily associates the stifling heat down here with the temperature presumably maintained in the heating system of Satan's apartments. It is the sheerest drop known, this from Jerusalem to Jericho, more than three thousand feet within a distance of fifteen miles.

Or perhaps telling you to go to Jericho originates with a story recounted by Our Lord. A man once started to make this journey from Jerusalem and "fell in with robbers, who after both stripping him and beating him went their way, leaving him half-dead" (Luke 10:30). A priest passed and saw the poor man's sad plight; a levite came on the scene and stared for a moment; but neither of them could be bothered so they just did nothing and continued on their way. It was not till a Samaritan arrived, one of the traditional enemies of the Jews, that things got going. The

Samaritan was moved to compassion, bound up the man's wounds, placed him on his own horse and brought him along to the inn. "Which of these three proved himself neighbor to him who fell among the robbers?" (Luke 10:36).

The only inn ever known along that route is still standing, on the site of the ancient inn. There are some who maintain it is the identical one referred to by Our Lord. We visited it. What caught our attention was the abundance of barbed wire in evidence. The inn is now used as a police barracks to afford protection to travellers, for that stretch of lonely country has never had an enviable reputation. We forgot to ask if it figured much in the recent disturbances between Jews and Arabs, but one surmises that it probably did.

CITY OF PALMS

In Our Lord's time Jericho was called the city of palms, and to this day the slogan goes that "Jericho is always green." This fertile plain near the Jordan is a refreshing sight after one's eyes for days have rested on nothing but the parched country in and around Jerusalem. It used to be a busy center too, for people travelling to Jerusalem had to check in here when coming from Galilee or Peraea, much as we have to go through the customs ourselves when passing from one country into another. The Customs' Officer in Jericho was named Zachaeus, a diminutive man whose story is forever linked with the Gospel narrative.

One evening, at the peak-point of the season, when the office was crammed to the door with visitors and a queue was chafing impatiently in line outside, word trickled in that Jesus of Nazareth had been observed in the town, passing through on His way down for the Paschal Feast.

Zachaeus pricked up his ears. Like everyone else he was consumed with the desire to see this Prophet and Wonder-Worker of Whom the whole countryside was talking. Here was a chance; he might never get another. Was there a side entrance to the Customs' Office, I wonder, and did he slip out that way unobserved? At any rate what Our Lord saw when He drew near was this highly respectable citizen astride the branch of a sycamore tree. The little man was lost in the crowd and could not see over the heads of the others, so, flinging human respect to the winds, he climbed up here, held on for dear life to the bough, caring not at all for the raillery he drew upon himself. He could see and that was all he wanted.

Our Lord beckoned to him to come down, and surely He was smiling, and He actually invited Himself to dinner in the house of the hated tax-gatherer. The grand people strutted around and swelled with indignation that they had been ignored, but Zachaeus, in a transport of delight, proceeded to conduct Jesus into his house. And even at this short notice he managed to prepare a splendid meal for the Guest Who had deigned to invite Himself—because probably Zachaeus would never have presumed of himself to proffer the invitation.

Jesus was no respecter of persons. Nor is He now.

FOUNTAIN OF ELISEUS

There were others also in Jericho who longed to see Jesus. Two men who were sitting near the city gate as He was passing out fell down on their knees, joined both hands together and implored Him to have mercy on them. What did they want Him to do? Of course He knew what the answer would be. The two poor men were blind and were certain to ask for a cure. But it is love's way to wish to hear the request made and to be gladdened by the trust that prompts it. What did they want? "Lord," replied each in turn, "that I may see!" (Luke 18:41). So He touched those poor sightless eyes and the scales dropped from them, and to their inexpressible delight they found themselves looking straight into the beautiful face of Jesus of Nazareth.

"Lord, that I may see!" Wasn't it the prayer that had brought us all this distance, nearly three thousand miles, that with the eye of faith we too might be able to discern Him?

About a mile to the south we stopped at the Fountain of Eliseus, just beside the ruins of Old Jericho. The prophet of old seems to have felt the attraction of this beautiful place, for he was wont to come here often. On the occasion of one of his visits the citizens assembled to present him with a pressing petition. The water had become bitter and impossible to drink and they begged the man of God to do something about it. Men of God, to this day as of old, are sometimes a little disconcerting, and the Jerichonians must have looked askance at each other when Eliseus asked for a fistful of salt. It was brought to him, and he threw it into the pool, and, contrary to what you might expect, it healed the waters and healed they remain to this day. The fountain, we were told, yields one thousand gallons a minute.

You never saw a more picturesque scene than presented itself to our eyes on reaching that fountain. It was late afternoon, with a glorious sunset in a blue sky. By unanimous consent we stopped the bus and I think we would willingly have spent the remainder of the evening here. Arab refugees from Israel have built a huge settlement in the vicinity of the fountain, and just now the whole place was all agog with movement. Scores of Arab women in flowing robes formed a sea of color as they passed in endless procession to and from the fountain with their pitchers on their heads. Hundreds of boys and girls, of all sizes and ages, played in the large field. The men talked together and smoked leisurely, leaving the women to do the work. We gathered it was near tea-time and preparations were being made amidst a buzz of ceaseless chatter interrupted by an occasional joke and a laugh and a smile.

NO PICTURES!

I felt really sorry for our photographers. The whole setting made a stunningly fine picture and seemed irresistible. But a rigid law forbade all taking of photos. The temptation was strong indeed, and one or two of our party ventured furtively to play the ominous camera on the group. But vigilant little boys shrieked out vigorous protests, pointed an accusing finger, and fetched the police! So, reluctantly, we drove on, trying to look very penitent and promising we would never do it again. We could take away this wonderful living picture, but only in our imagination. Nor did we feel the slightest resentment; the unwillingness of these good people to be "snapped," under the circumstances, is very intelligible.

Old Jericho is at present being excavated by the Americans. A few miles beyond it we went to the foot of the Mount of Temptation which is pointed out as the place where the devil carried Our Lord and tempted Him by showing Him all the kingdoms of the world. "All these will I give thee, if thou wilt fall down and worship me" (Matt. 4:9). It is a high barren mountain; on the slope about halfway up, the Greek Orthodox have a monastery and church. Thence on to the Dead Sea, where a few of our party had a swim. It is possible to stand only in very shallow water. The chemicals leave you with a sharp pain in the eyes, but the swim is most refreshing, though it is only with considerable difficulty that you manage to plunge. We saw an immense deposit of salt on the banks. The tradition is that the ruins of Sodom and

Gomorrha, the two cities of sin, having been destroyed by fire, were buried in the depths of this sea.

We drove back to Jerusalem along the desert road in the moonlight. We passed the inn of the Good Samaritan again, and through the lighted windows saw groups of soldiers with red headdress, seated at the tables, probably playing cards.

WALLS OF JERICHO

The walls of Old Jericho figure in an Old Testament story. It came back to my mind, and in a very particular setting. A young priest was preparing to go out to give his first public mission. "Any hints you can give me, Father?" he asked a seasoned old veteran. And between them they recalled the incidents surrounding the fall of the walls of Jericho. Josue, leader of the Israelites, was laying siege to the city which the Lord had promised to deliver into his hands.

"Go round about the city," he was told, "all ye fighting men, once a day: so shall ye do for six days. And on the seventh day . . . you shall go about the city seven times . . . and the walls of the city shall fall to the ground. So all the people making a shout, and the trumpets sounding, when the voice and the sound thundered forth in the ears of the multitude, the walls forthwith fell down" (Josue 6:3, 4, 5, 20).

But what had all this to do with the young priest's first mission? Well, the soul, explained the old man, is like Jericho. Many who come to your mission have been resisting God's grace, probably for a long time. Other missioners have made the attempt. They have marched around the walls raised by sin about that soul. But now, please God, the mission has begun, during which those walls will at last fall to the ground and God's grace will enter and take possession.

Whatever be the point of telling you to go to Jericho I feel certain that all of us, if ever again we are given that recommendation, will be very glad to be able to say we've been there, but thank you very much all the same!

12. *Out at Bethany*

Everybody likes to be made to feel at home. Especially if you have been living amidst strangers do you appreciate at once the change of atmosphere when you find yourself again surrounded by those you love and who love you. And if those strangers have been, not merely aloof, but suspicious of you, hostile, scrutinizing your every word in order to twist it as evidence against you, you know how you will draw a long breath of relief when at last you get back home and can relax.

Our divine Lord loved Bethany because it was the nearest thing to home after Mary and Nazareth. Up in Jerusalem enemies watched Him narrowly, lynx-eyed to put evil construction on His actions, carping at every word He spoke in order to catch Him. Their warped minds were poisoned by envy, and implacable hatred had changed their hearts to granite. Was it any wonder that He sometimes longed to get away from this constant bickering and quibbling?

Out at Bethany, less than a mile from the city, near Cedron, to the southeast, there lived a little family who had a welcome for Him always and He knew it. It was sanctuary. Here there was perfect harmony, here was mutual understanding, and the human heart in Him, wearied by the perversity it met with in men who refused to see, here tasted sweet consolation. For friends were here and their eyes would light up with a joy they made no attempt to disguise every time they saw Him walk in the door.

MEET THE FAMILY

The door is gone, of course, and the little house with it. But the Franciscans have built a church, within recent years, on the site. It was good to be here, good to kneel in yet another spot where the feet of the Saviour had stood, good to calm the tumult in one's heart, and in prayer recapture the peace Christ had experienced here—for it does linger, even today, in this hallowed spot.

There were three in the family at Bethany: two sisters named Mary and Martha, and their brother Lazarus. One gets the impression from the Gospel story that Lazarus was of a quiet, retiring nature. He seems to keep in the background whenever visitors were about. At any rate, if he was present, he apparently decided to leave all the talking to the women, showing in this, perhaps, a wisdom beyond his years!

We have no record of a single word that fell from his lips and we might have almost forgotten his existence were it not for the graphic story in which he was destined to play a leading rôle. Jesus loved Lazarus dearly. There is a whole world of pathos in the scene described by St. John where he shows us Our Lord standing by the grave of Lazarus and weeping bitter tears for the death of His friend.

We too went out to that grave, only a few hundred yards from the church. A little old man heard us approaching and rather startled us by emerging, slowly and with some difficulty, from the very mouth of the tomb. The gradual sight of him was a vivid reminder of the miracle wrought here by Our Blessed Lord. The difficulty he had in getting out was due to his age and consequent slowness of gait, not to the smallness of the exit. For he too was low-sized and rotund, not in the least like what we fancied Lazarus to be.

He has been in and out of that tomb thousands of times, for he has been in charge for more than fifty-five years. Sure, it's a lifetime, and could you imagine him ever forgetting the Scripture's injunction: "In all thy works remember thy last end, and thou shalt never sin?" (Ecclus. 7:40). He was alive and full of talk, all keyed up to tell us everything about the place and show us round. At the end we induced him to stand in a group with us and be photographed.

"HE WHOM THOU LOVEST"

There was consternation in the Bethany household when Lazarus took ill. The two sisters instinctively thought of their friend, but He was across the Jordan, about a day's journey away, and they were probably loath to intrude. But the sick man's condition grew worse, so at last they sent messengers to the Master to say: "He whom thou lovest is sick" (John 11:3). No need to mention him by name; Jesus would understand; He always did; He always does. Neither do they ask for a cure; they do not suggest that Our Lord should come away from whatever important business is detaining Him and journey down to little Bethany. They merely lay the case before Him, never doubting that He would do about it whatever was best.

He did, but not for four whole days after the young man was dead and buried. Mustn't it have been hard for Him, loving as He did, to stay His eagerness to give immediate consolation and thus appear as if He was indifferent to their great sorrow? Doesn't He seem to treat our own trusting and persevering prayers like this too? The delay in granting comfort to Martha and Mary would enhance for all subsequent time the steadfastness of the confidence they placed in Him.

For, when finally they learn that He is at last on the way to them, first Martha, and then Mary her sister in turn come out of the house to meet Him, and each, independently of the other, addresses Him in the same words: "Lord, if thou hadst been here, my brother would not have died" (John 11:21, 32). And Jesus said: "Where have you laid him?" (John 11:33). They say to him: " 'Lord, come and see.' And Jesus wept. The Jews therefore said, 'See how he loved him.' . . . When he had said this, he cried out with a loud voice, 'Lazarus, come forth.' And at once he who had been dead came forth, bound feet and hands with bandages, and his face was tied up with a cloth. Jesus said to them, 'Unbind him, and let him go.' " (John 11:35–36, 43–44).

SUCH WASTE!

Our Lord spent the last week of His life with them here, a brief spell of tranquillity before the impending storm. St. John describes what happened, in his twelfth chapter. The family of Our Lord's friends seems determined to do things in a big way. Martha has the supper prepared, and Lazarus, whom He raised from the dead, is with Him at the table. Martha's contribution would be the excellent meal, and the very presence of Lazarus would be enough to proclaim his gratitude and to make acknowledgment of the divine power that called him from the grave.

And Mary—what tribute could she bring to grace the occasion, and to give expression to the love that filled her heart? She "took a pound of ointment, genuine nard of great value, and anointed the feet of Jesus, and with her hair wiped his feet dry. And the house was filled with the odor of the ointment" (3). There are those who might consider it a rather meaningless gesture. It did not serve any useful purpose, this extravagant pouring out of ointment by this senseless, unreflecting woman. There was good money going down the drain!

The criticism was expressed, though disguised under the cloak of religion; and it is very significant that it came from the lips of Judas Iscariot who was about to betray Him. Judas carried the purse and could not smother the sorrow of his avaricious heart as he sat and watched the action of Mary. That ointment should have been sold; it would fetch three hundred pence, and what a substantial alms that would be for the poor! We may well believe that if that money had once got into the greedy grasp of Judas it would never have found its way into the home of any poor person. He was angry that the money had gone astray and feels he must make a showing of righteousness for his anger.

The echo of that complaint is often heard still. There are those who pose as friends of the poor, who affect to be scandalized at the extravagance lavished on the Church and her ceremonial, in her effort to give to God the praise and glory that are His due. To what purpose is this waste? Is Judas their progenitor?

Our Lord undertakes to defend Mary's action. "The poor you have always with you, but you do not always have me" (John 12:8).

There were several very interested spectators who began to arrive when they heard that Jesus was in Bethany. They had a double motive for coming—not only to meet Our Lord, but also to see Lazarus whom He had raised from the dead. This desire to contact and observe what is miraculous and spectacular is never enough, of itself, for genuine conversion. The Kingdom does not need outward enthusiasm which is fed by mere emotion, but inward conviction, the action of divine faith and grace on the soul of him who seeks. Many seek in religion mere satisfaction of their feelings. When pleasant feelings and spiritual delights evaporate, their religion too begins to decline. Their seeking of God and religion is not without admixture of self-love. They come "not only because of Jesus, but that they might see Lazarus, whom he had raised from the dead" (John 12:9).

ONE THING NECESSARY

There is still another Bethany scene which must be indicated. He called one evening and Martha bustled about the house, all preoccupied to make sure there would be a nice meal. But Mary wasn't interested. It looks indeed as if she did not even remember that a meal would be required, because all she did was to settle herself at the Master's feet, sit down there engrossed, her eyes fixed on Him, every word He spoke striking a chord of immediate response in her heart. Now was this a fair division? Certainly Martha did not think it was. So she stands before Christ and her sister, and, expanding both arms wide, proceeds to expostulate. "Lord, is it no concern of thine that my sister has left me to serve alone? Tell her therefore to help me" (Luke 10:40).

It does surely seem a just complaint. Still, the

Lord undertakes to defend Mary. "Martha," He says, and for emphasis repeats the name, "Martha, thou art anxious and troubled about many things, and yet only one thing is needful. Mary has chosen the best part, and it will not be taken away from her" (Luke 10:41–42).

Excessive activity and restless agitation will undoubtedly sap the taste of the soul for prayer and the things of the spirit. St. Bernard wrote a lengthy treatise to Pope Eugenius (formerly a monk in Bernard's monastery). It dealt with "Consideration," and the saint went to great lengths to impress upon the Pope the absolute necessity of separating himself, at very frequent and regular intervals, from the multitude of external business matters. If he permits himself to live in a state of constant turmoil he will be overwhelmed with material cares, and even with spiritual ones, but he will lose his love of prayer and his power of concentrating seriously on the things of God.

St. Bernard was ahead of his time. It is becoming increasingly difficult nowadays to escape from noise and plunge into the apartness where prayer between God and the soul deepens. Most of us spend our time looking out; Christ defended Mary because she is one of the rare souls who take time off to look in, into the marvels of the life of grace, the life that matters, which is developing in the secret places of each soul. This is the one thing necessary, the life which abides, which shall not be taken away.

13. *Mount Thabor*

Mount Thabor has been compared to a massive High Altar raised up by God for the glorification of His divine Son. It rises, awe-inspiring in its sheer majesty, from the valley surrounding it and dominated by it, till it reaches the height of nearly two thousand feet above the level of the Mediterranean. On the summit, on a wide plateau, to commemorate the Transfiguration of Jesus Christ, the Franciscans have erected a church—a thing of beauty in the simplicity of its Syrian design, sculptured, without columns, restrained in its ornamentation. The cost of this magnificent basilica was defrayed by the Catholics of the United States.

The psalmist foresaw that this colossal mountain would leap for joy, exulting in the Name of the Lord. This prophecy was fulfilled on that never-to-be-forgotten day, when Our Lord, taking with Him His three disciples, Peter, James, and John, "was transfigured before them. And his face shone as the sun, and his garments became white as snow" (Matt. 17:2). "And behold, a voice out of the cloud said, 'This is my beloved Son, in whom I am well pleased;

hear him" (Matt. 17:5). We had been privileged to follow after Him, tracing His footsteps up along that zigzag pathway, right up to the top of this "high mountain apart." It must have taken Him several hours to climb. We went by car in about twenty minutes. It was a somewhat unnerving experience, up on those dizzy heights, swerving and lurching suddenly from one side to the other, and those of us who made the return journey also by car were even more terrified. All, however, survived to tell the tale.

THY PEOPLE ISRAEL

The Friars, thoughtful as ever, suggested that perhaps we would like to have Benediction up here, with the Blessed Sacrament exposed. Of course we eagerly accepted the offer. It was like the Transfiguration all over again. "Jesus Christ, yesterday, today, and the same forever," exposed in that monstrance, was right in our midst, just as He was on that memorable day of the Transfiguration, and it needed no great effort to catch once again the voice of the heavenly Father giving testimony: "This is my beloved Son, in whom I am well pleased."

You could not but reflect on the beauty and consolation of the Catholic faith. Here are thirty-eight

Irish pilgrims, absolutely convinced, and on grounds that must appeal to the reason of every thinking person, that they are at this moment kneeling in adoration before the Son of God. "Lord, it is good for us to be here" (Matt. 17:4). Peter had said it first here on Thabor, and today his words came back to our minds and found a ringing echo in our hearts. A Protestant once confided to a Catholic friend of mine: "If I believed what you Catholics believe about the Blessed Eucharist, I think I'd never be off my knees."

When the venerable old man Simeon had taken Christ into his arms in the Temple—Mary, the Child's mother, had brought Him there to be presented to the Lord—his face shone with happiness for he recognized in Him the long-promised Messias. He proclaimed Him to be "a light of revelation to the Gentiles, and a glory for thy people Israel" (Luke 2:32).

A young Jewish boy was attending a Catholic school. During religious instruction each day he was sent into a room by himself and given some poetry to memorize. One day, quite by accident, he came upon a copy of the New Testament and, by way of varying his rather dull program, looked through the pages. The more he read the more absorbed he became. He had discovered a treasure, the existence of which he

Franciscan Church on Mount Thabor

Haifa and Mount Carmel

had hitherto not even suspected. It took some years for the seed thus sown to take root and bring forth fruit, but finally he became convinced of the claims of Jesus Christ and entered the Catholic Church.

"Thy people Israel." At the solemn moment of imparting the Benediction the priest on Thabor holds that same Christ, and from this dazzling eminence they both look down with love on His "people Israel," there at His feet. Alas, that they are not prostrate there, that multitudes of them consider it would be disloyalty, almost blasphemy, to open the New Testament and at least investigate the reasons why He said He was God. The eyes of His people have been turned away from the true Light and their heart is estranged from Him by love of this world's tinsel. "I have spread forth my hands all day to an unbelieving people, who walk in a way that is not good, after their own thoughts (Isai. 65:2).

MOSES AND ELIAS

In the happiness and certainty of our Catholic faith we knelt and adored Him, and bowed our heads low as He lifted His hands to bless us. After Benediction we joined in singing our hymn, and Mount Thabor heard the strains of "Faith of Our Fathers."

How one longed to share this priceless treasure, gathering into this venerable sanctuary His entire people where they might discover for themselves "the Holy One of Israel!"

On this mountain too there appeared with Our Lord Moses and Elias. Moses is the representative of the Law, and Jesus had come, not to destroy the Law, but to fulfill it. Elias, one of the major prophets, is seen with Our Lord, to indicate that in Christ all the prophecies are accomplished. "Search the Scriptures," He had challenged the Jews of His time, "it is they that bear witness to me" (John 5:39). Catholicism is not the denial of Jewry any more than the flower is the negation of the root from which it springs.

Moses and Elias have each a special chapel up here, and we knelt before their statues to pray. There is also a very fine painting over the High Altar showing the Transfiguration scene.

The view from this height baffles description. When you come out from the church and look over to your left, there stretches away for miles the Plain of Esdraelon, and, further still, Little Hermon and Mount Carmel. To your right, toward the north, you have the giant Hermon, always covered with snow, and the mountain ranges Hauran and Safed toward north and south respectively; the whole is interspersed with towns and villages, basking in a wonderful sunshine. Here is a surpassingly lovely landscape, with Christ in the tabernacle looking down upon it all, and but a few minutes ago raining upon it and its people—His people Israel—the plenitude of His blessing.

ONLY JESUS

Peter, intoxicated with joy at the vision of the transfigured Christ, cried out that he would wish to build here three tabernacles, one for Our Lord, one for Moses, and one for Elias, "not knowing what he said" (Luke 9:33). Even a momentary breaking through of the splendor of the divinity, ordinarily hidden underneath the veils of the sacred humanity, causes those favored apostles to be transported with happiness. What then to possess God, not for a fleeting moment, but to hold Him fast with the assurance that no power on earth or in hell can take Him from one?

But Thabor was only a blinding flash, intended to confirm these same three men when presently they would follow the Master to Gethsemani and see Him crushed and humiliated. "Lifting up their eyes, they saw no one but Jesus only" (Matt. 17:8).

"Only Jesus"—an excellent ideal for the living of a

truly Christian life. For in the Catholic all men should lift up their eyes and see another transfiguration. His standards adhered to in our business methods, in our social life; His love, the logical outcome of knowing Him intimately, influencing us in our dealings with our fellowmen; His very life, indeed, communicated to our souls in baptism, waxing stronger each day; His approval alone sought for; the rewards promised by Him the one object of our striving—this is part of what "only Jesus" would mean in our daily lives if in them He held the place due to Him on a thousand counts.

"And as they were coming down from the mountain, Jesus cautioned them, saying, 'Tell the vision to no one, till the Son of Man has risen from the dead' " (Matt. 17:9). Two priests walked down from that mountain together that day and talked of many interesting things. One of them was a missionary who is devoting his life to working for the conversion of "His people Israel"; the other is the author of this book. My friend remarked that it is good to be alive in times like the present, when the Church has to have Catholics of grit, men and women of fighting spirit, men and women who are ready to suffer and die for the Faith—a sentiment that recalled similar noble words spoken by the lion-hearted Pope Pius XI. This priest once said that in the course of casual conversation. A girl in the company heard it, and could not put it from her mind. Six months later she returned to tell the priest that his words were haunting her, and she had decided to become a nun. And a splendid nun she is at this moment.

APOSTOLATE

My companion was four times condemned to death because of his known sympathy with the Jews. When he told me that, I noted it mentally and promised myself to bring him back to it and hear the details. Alas, we talked about other things and it slipped my memory. He is never done asking for prayers and sacrifices for this people, in whom he discerns characteristics which, if directed, would mould them into magnificent Catholics. Up and down through Israel there are little groups of Catholics, thoroughly imbued with the apostolic spirit. These form the leaven, and, please God, in time they and those who inherit their spirit will leaven the whole mass. They meet regularly in New Jerusalem to have a spiritual retreat and discuss their problems and seek advice.

It is an apostolate demanding inexhaustible patience. This is the sowing-time. Another will reap the harvest, but only on condition that now the seed is cast into the ground. "Unless the grain of wheat falls into the ground and dies, it remains alone. But if it dies, it brings forth much fruit" (John 12:24).

Significantly enough, when Moses and Elias appeared up here on Thabor with Christ, they were speaking of his death, "which he was about to fulfill in Jerusalem" (Luke 9:31). You might regard this as a jarring note introduced at the moment when He is being glorified. But the fact is that the glory of Thabor may never be separated, even in thought, from the humiliation of Calvary. One complements the other.

This is true of the spiritual life of each individual, to whom Christ will sometimes grant abundance of sweetness in His service, and sometimes plunge into darkness and desolation, when everything seems completely confused. It is true of His Church, whose history alternates between Thabor and Calvary. It is true of Israel, all these centuries deprived of the Light of the World, "seated in darkness and in the shadow of death," and destined soon, perhaps, to emerge from the night and exult in the knowledge and love of Christ transfigured before it.

14. *The Cenacle*

It was a very pleasant surprise to learn we were going to visit the room of the Last Supper. I had somehow got the idea that it was not included in our itinerary. I was very glad to hear that this was a mistake, though the visit, one has to admit, turned out to be something of a disappointment.

And why? Well, to begin with, there is not a vestige left of the original room. All has been completely destroyed and the site is now occupied by a mosque. We were told that the ground floor formerly consisted of a harem for Moslem widows; when you climb up the stairs outside, which leads to the second story, you reach the so-called Tomb of David. The Jews maintain that David is buried here, though there are strong arguments against the belief. We visited the Tomb, having been warned to keep our hats on, as a mark of respect! It is simply a long vault dug into a wall, with lights burning in front, railed in, and guarded by a Moslem soldier. Seven crowns lie on the tomb, one for each year of the liberation of the Jews. We weren't impressed, I'm afraid, more especially as the place is of more than doubtful authenticity.

REALITY AGAIN

On the same floor you have what is now known as the Cenacle, built in the same position and site where stood the original room of the Last Supper. It is about forty feet long, unfurnished, uncarpeted, without seats or chairs or pictures or decoration of any sort. Time was when Christians dared not even kneel here, to pray in such a hallowed spot, without being jeered at by Turks or Mohammedans. As a prominent Jew in Israel did not fail to point out to us, since the coming into being of the new state all Christians are now free to remain in this sacred place as long as they wish, and to perform any private devotions without interference.

So what you had to do was to shut your eyes and black out the memory of what was accidental and focus your thoughts on the astounding reality. It is a mere accident that the original room is gone, an accident that the entire place is in the hands of strangers, and that, much as we longed, we could not say Mass here or receive Holy Communon, where, on Holy Thursday night, Our Lord gave us the Blessed Eucharist. These were the things we had to try to forget.

And what to remember? To remember that the Son of God had climbed up a stairs like the one that still leads to this room, built, not in the house, as ours at home, but on the outside; that He had come into this very spot, had girt Himself with a towel, taken a basin of water, and knelt to wash the feet of His disciples; that here He ate the Pasch with them, and while seated at table, here took bread and wine and celebrated the first Mass, changing these elements into His Body and Blood; that here, on this blessed night, He ordained His first priests, entrusting to their frail keeping the stupendous power to do what He Himself had just done; that here, after the Ascension, they returned, persevering with Mary in prayer, making what might be called the first enclosed retreat; that on the morning their retreat ended, the Spirit of God descended upon them, in the form of tongues of fire, and sat upon every one of them; that here, finally, as tradition states, Mary's death occurred, and the apostles carried her body to the grave outside, and buried it in the present "Church of the Dormition."

RECONSTRUCTION

What a host of hallowed memories! Imagination would insist on reconstructing the scene. During the days immediately preceding the Pasch and Last Supper Our Lord was out at Bethany, probably at the house of Martha and Mary and Lazarus. He sent in the two apostles Peter and John to the city to prepare for the festival. You could easily envisage them walking the street and on the lookout for a man carrying on his head a pitcher of water. Our Lord had explained that this man would tell them how to find the way to the Cenacle. A man with a pitcher on his head would have been an unusual spectacle, quickly to be noticed, for it is nearly always the women who draw the water.

So they would have met the man, stopped him and questioned him, and he would have told them the place was over here on the south side of the city. They found the way easily enough after that, climbed up the stone stairs outside, came in here and saw that the room was furnished and that everything was in readiness. An hour or two later, Jesus Himself would have come and the rest of the disciples with Him. In their turn they too would have mounted that flight of steps, entered into this room, found their places at the table, and sat down here where we were now privileged to kneel. "Now when evening arrived, he reclined at table with the twelve disciples" (Matt. 26:20).

THE GIVING OF CHRIST

We read aloud St. Luke's inspired account. "And when the hour had come, he reclined at table, and the twelve apostles with him. And he said to them, 'I have greatly desired to eat this passover with you before I suffer. . . . And having taken a cup, he gave thanks and said, 'Take this and share it among you. . . . And having taken bread, he gave thanks and broke, and gave it to them, saying, 'This is my body, which is being given for you; do this in remembrance of me.' In like manner he took also the cup after the supper, saying, 'This cup is the new covenant in my blood, which shall be shed for you. But behold, the hand of him who betrays me is with me on the table' " (Luke 22:14–21). "This is my blood," writes St. Matthew, "of the new covenant, which is being shed for many unto the forgiveness of sins" (Matt. 26:28).

Three salient truths impressed themselves as we knelt together here in prayer. There was first the gift itself. God gives us God; omnipotence, so to say, is here taxing its powers, for what greater than Himself could even God give to men? "Rejoice and praise, O thou habitation of Sion, for great is He that is in the midst of thee, the Holy One of Israel." Secondly, there was the peculiar circumstance of the time chosen by Our Lord to give. For He gives on the very night He will be betrayed, when "the hand of him who betrays me is with me on the table." It is a pleasure to distribute gifts and favors to those whose love and loyalty we have tested and found true. But it takes divine love to press its benefits on those who have spurned its love. Furthermore, Our Lord knows that this is His last night with them, and that it is natural for us to lay stress on the value of a present we receive as a parting gift. Finally, Jesus gives and surrounds the giving with circumstances to prove the willingness with which He gives. So much depends on how we give. Give unwillingly, give and complain while you give, give and cast your gift grudgingly into the hands of him who needs it, insinuating that you hope he will not ask again—to give like this is, in very large measure, to destroy the value of your gift. Our Lord "having loved his own who were in the world, loved them to the end," and gives in such a manner as to enhance, if possible, a gift already infinite in value.

As you knelt there, you thought of the washing of the feet, of the exquisite discourse He spoke imme-diately after their Holy Communion, of the ardent prayer He sent up to the heavenly Father begging Him to protect them from evil, seeing that He was now about to leave them, and that they must go out into the world to preach His Gospel. The whole setting in which He deigns to give them the Gift is deliberately ordered with a view to emphasizing the Gift of the Lover and the love of the Giver.

THE FUTURE?

I'm nearly certain we were told that a Catholic priest had been able to offer the Holy Sacrifice here in recent times. Hopes are rising that this Cenacle, sacred to us for so many reasons, may once more pass into Catholic hands. In its present condition it is one of the big disappointments the Catholic pilgrim must face, but still we would not have missed this visit for worlds. Every Holy Thursday there is a constant stream of Christian pilgrims who come hither in order to make grateful commemoration of this Gift, given at such a time, and in such a manner.

They come like hungry children seeking bread, the Bread of Life that came down from heaven. It is a place where they have every right to expect to find It. But the granaries are empty. They turn in here like travellers in the dark night to discover a light that will cheer them and guide them along the road home. But the sanctuary lamp is out, and there is nobody here to pour in more oil. In their loneliness they draw near to speak to a Friend Who never yet has failed them. This should indeed be His home, but the altar is gone and the tabernacle is thrown down. There is no Real Presence; only a Real Absence.

The climb up here is very stiff; there must surely be about two hundred steps in sections of fives and sixes. Our guide was adamant that it would be too great a tax on the strength of some of our party and they were told to remain below. They did not like this a bit and their protests were easy to understand. It was not hard to sympathize with them when, finding themselves within sight of the Promised Land, they were forbidden to enter.

And perhaps that is as fitting a description as any other of the Cenacle, that it is a Promised Land. Is the day far distant when Catholics may enter it, not as it were by stealth and on sufferance, but freely and in full light of day? Is the hour approaching when the Eucharistic Sacrifice first offered here by Our Lord will be continued from the rising of the sun till the going down of the same? Is it too much to hope that, at no very distant date, Christian and Jew will kneel here side by side, feeding at the same Table, their hearts closely welded in love and in faith, recognizing Him in the breaking of bread?

"How can this man give us his flesh to eat?" (John 6:53). It was the question that baffled the Jews of old, when first He made this promise. It was a hard saying which they could not accept; so many of them turned and went their way and walked no more with Him. It is a marvellous tribute to the Catholic Faith that over four hundred million Catholics, and perhaps another hundred million Orthodox Christians, all believe in the Real Presence, convinced that He is there, because He says He is, even though no man can answer adequately how this can be. Only God could demand such faith and Christ does demand it and can, because He is God.

15. *The Night Before*

Please imagine that you have just come out of the garden at Gethsemani. In front of you is the city of Jerusalem, enclosed by four walls which make a rough square. This is the eastern wall here straight before you, and we would ask you to let your eye run along the full length of it in the direction of your left hand, till, less than a mile down, it joins at right angles the extremity of the southern wall. Now suppose you turn that corner and walk up by the wall skirting the southern side of the town. If you do, you will presently find yourself beside the Cenacle, the room of the Last Supper which we entered in spirit in our last chapter.

So if on that Holy Thursday night you had taken up a position here, with the garden behind you, and had looked across toward your left hand, you would have been able, easily enough, to pick out the procession of Christ and His eleven apostles coming from the city over to where you are standing. Judas is the twelfth apostle, but he is not here; at this very moment he is making final arrangements with Our Lord's enemies for the arrest. "Whomever I kiss, that is he; lay hold of him" (Matt. 26:48).

WORDS OF FIRE

From where you wait you discern the figure of Jesus Christ, a little in advance of the others and with head bent slightly forward, His long white flowing garment shimmering in the rays of the full moon overhead. We were most anxious, during our pilgrimage, to cover this exact route trodden by the Master as He walked down from the Cenacle to the garden. But it was impossible. Gethsemani is in Jordan and the Supper Room is in Israel, and a "no man's land" lies between.

They are walking rather slowly, you observe, as men are wont to walk when deep in conversation. They halt occasionally, and the little group presses in around Him, looking up at Him, full in the face, eager to hear what He has to tell them. Sometimes He emphasizes with a gesture the importance of what He says, raising, now the index finger of the right hand, and again one or both arms, from the shoulder, as though with added forcefulness to drive the message home.

To speak in our human way Our divine Lord "lets

Himself go" tonight. It is His last night with those men whom He has called His "little children," and never before did He so tax His powers of eloquence in the effort to hold the attention of those children and make them understand. He seems to be grappling with words. They must come to grips with the truth that when He tells them His heart is on fire with love for them, He is stating a simple fact.

We can never be grateful enough to St. John for preserving for us a detailed account of that marvellous conversation. For all time is enshrined in the great final chapters of his Gospel, an inexhaustible source from which to draw material for our prayer. On the road to Emmaus, after His Resurrection, Jesus overtook two of His disciples and talked to them and their hearts burned within them while He spoke to them on the way. Can we doubt that the same happened in this room on the night before His death? As they journeyed to Emmaus, Our Lord, "beginning with Moses and with all the prophets . . . interpreted to them in all the Scriptures the things referring to himself" (Luke 24:22). It is difficult not to regret that no record has come down to us of that interpretation.

But we are more fortunate in the account we possess of the conversation after the Last Supper.

Much of the fragrance of those last chapters in St. John will be regained and long linger, if we meditate on the sentences embodying the three ideas, which, like a refrain, run through the entire discourse.

THREE TRUTHS

It is hard to keep from at least indicating how this can be done. Our Lord is telling them, first, that they have no understanding of the depth of the personal love He bears each one of them. Listen to this: "I will not leave you orphans; I will come to you" (John 14:18). "As the Father has loved me, I also have loved you. . . . No longer do I call you servants, because the servant does not know what his master does. But I have called you friends, because all things that I have heard from my Father I have made known to you" (John 15:9, 15).

Side by side with this, there is His yearning for a return of love. "If you love me, keep my commandments" (John 14:15). "If anyone love me, he will keep my word, and my Father will love him, and we will come to him and make our abode with him" (John 14:23). "As the Father has loved me, I also have loved you. Abide in my love" (John 15:9).

He gives them what He calls His own special commandment: "This is my commandment, that you love one another as I have loved you" (John 15:12). "By this will all men know that you are my disciples, if you have love for one another" (John 13:35). "These things I command you, that you may love one another" (John 15:17). "Holy Father, keep in thy name those whom thou hast given me, that they may be one even as we are" (John 17:11).

Could they walk this road tonight and listen to such outpourings, and their hearts not burn within them? Happy for those who lived in such intimate contact with Him, who not only heard these words as they actually fell from His lips, but also thrilled to the ring of sincerity and conviction of the tones in which they were spoken! But was it so difficult after all, as you stood here in front of the garden, to see the whole scene re-enacted and once more catch His accents as He speaks about love—His love for them; their love for Him; the bond of mutual love between themselves which is to prove that they love Him indeed?

"KNOWING ALL THINGS . . ."

As they draw nearer to you, the rays of the moon fall across the face of Christ. You start at the sight. For you now observe that there is upon Him a frightened, hunted look. Come down from the garden as far as the brook Cedron and walk over that little bridge with Him. Why, the Man's eyes are stark with terror. The whole frame of Him is trembling. Yet nobody has laid a finger upon Him since He left the Supper room and began this walk in the moonlight and entered upon this entrancing conversation.

Once again He speaks, but this time there is a strained tone, and His words come in an unnatural voice. "My soul is sad, even unto death. Wait here and watch with me" (Matt. 26:38). And he goes forward a stone's throw and falls down on His knees and prays. Kneel beside Him and pray with Him. As you do, to your dismay, He falls flat on His face and writhes in anguish. Rest your hands on those trembling shoulders, at least to steady Him. Your hands? Stand up. Come out into the moonlight and look at your hands. They are wet, wet with the Precious Blood that has just been forced out through the pores of His Body.

What ever can have happened to cause all this? Turn again to St. John's gospel and he will tell you about "Jesus . . . knowing all that was to come upon him . . ." (John 18:4).

Tomorrow is the Passion and this is the night before. He knows that you see.

16. *Gethsemani*

We had a Holy Hour one night in Gethsemani. Shortly after seven o'clock we set out in groups of three and four, making our way down through King David Street and leaving the city by the St. Stephen Gate. This gate marks the spot where Stephen, the first Christian martyr, was stoned to death. He had upbraided the Jews, in no measured terms, for their hardness of heart, telling them they were resisting the Spirit of God in refusing to accept the claims of Jesus Christ to be their God-made-Man. They were filled with anger and they kept pelting him with stones till he fell here and died. A prayer was on his dying lips, reminiscent of the plea that rose from the dying Saviour, "Lord, do not lay this sin against them" (Acts 7:60).

A young man named Saul, a staunch Jew, held the garments of the men who were stoning Stephen, and presumably urged them on. This man, trained in the rigid ways of the Pharisees in the school of Gamaliel, was later to be transformed into one of Our Lord's most ardent apostles, the immortal Paul. Judge how completely he was won to love of the Name of Christ from the fact that he writes it nearly three hundred times in his Epistles.

"WAIT HERE AND WATCH"

We halted here at this gate for a moment and looked over toward the Valley of Cedron on our left—the route followed by Our Lord when He climbed the Mount of Olives. Another time we would go there, but tonight we must take the opposite direction, on our right, leading to the Franciscan Church of All Nations, and the garden of Gethsemani beside it. We waited for each other at the entrance to the garden and in reverent silence prepared ourselves for this soul-searching experience. Who will say it is fantasy to see Him here in our midst, just as He had stood with that other group of His apostles? Or to hear again His invitation: "My soul is sad, even unto death. Wait here and watch with me. . . . Could you not watch one hour with me?" (Matt. 26:38, 40).

An atmosphere more conducive to prayer would be impossible to find. Here is a beautiful summer night, with full moon in a clear, blue sky; all around us the hushed silence of expectancy as we waited for the first act in the tremendous drama about to begin. Should we not cast the shoes off our feet before presuming to tread in the footsteps of the Master along this holy ground?

Everything was in readiness for us at the church; so we began without delay our hour of watching and praying. In front of the High Altar, railed in on four sides, is the large rock, still in position, against which Jesus Christ had leaned for support during that terrible agony. It was here that the vision rose up before His gaze of the sins of the world, and of the Passion He must undergo to expiate them. Here echoed in the tense silence the cry of anguish wrung from His Sacred Heart: "Father, if it is possible, let this cup pass away from me; yet not as I will, but as thou willest" (Matt. 26:39). Sweat broke out through the pores of His Body, saturated His garments, and, mixed with His Blood, fell down in great drops to the ground.

Of course for all of us the story had a familiar ring. But one single word in the account tonight makes a whole world of difference. Tonight it was "this" ground, not "the" ground. He had knelt here; here He lay flat on His face in a deadly hand-to-hand struggle with sin and the powers of evil; this is the earth, here, which on that night had drunk in His Precious Blood. And here He is still in the Blessed Eucharist, "Jesus Christ, yesterday, today, and the same forever."

If the reality of it all was too immense for our puny minds to grasp, at least we had answered His invitation to come here and spend this hour and make the attempt to appreciate the truth.

"DOST THOU BETRAY?"

We lingered in the little garden, to the right of the church as you face the city. Here stand, to this day, olive trees like those that had been silent witnesses of the Agony, probably offshoots of those growing there that night, possibly, say some authorities, the actual trees themselves. Our divine Lord had advanced thus far, from the site of the present church, to meet Judas in this place. Here the soldiers had fallen to the ground, overawed, it would seem, by the majesty of His bearing, and, though they did not know it, paralyzed by the nearness of the divinity in Him.

As He stands there now, all sign of fear has dropped from Him like a cloak. He is complete Master of the situation, although, naturally speaking, He should be the One to dread it most of all. Father Aidan McGrath, an Irish priest who suffered much at Communist hands, will tell you: "I am a coward. I assure you my knees used to knock together when I heard those men coming to take me." But he endured it all with heroic constancy—because he learned to pray. It is in prayer that our strength lies. It is from prayer that the Master draws His courage. And there is a note of deep concern tonight; here at our Holy Hour, as He warns us of the pitfalls prepared for us too by our enemies, He points to persevering prayer as the one weapon, more than all others, needed if we are to win through.

We had tried to sip, at least, His bitter chalice. We had essayed to learn, in this school of suffering love, what is the true nature of sin. Above all, we had engaged ourselves on the helpless, hopeless task of fathoming the infinite abyss of the love He bears us. His friends on Holy Thursday were asleep, for their eyes were heavy; His disciples, at the first appearance of danger, "left him and fled" (Matt. 26:56). And His enemies? Judas was not asleep, nor the men up in the city holding midnight council and plotting His capture and death. And today? Is history repeating itself? Certainly His enemies are not asleep; certainly they are not showing any sign of fear; there are those who consider them to be endowed with an energy that might be considered satanic. And His friends? Asleep? Apathetic?

The Holy Father's words are appropriate here:

Christians in the present hour, when the unity and peace of the world, and the very sources of life, are endangered, can only lift up their eyes towards the Virgin, who now appears clothed in powerful regality. How We could wish that all those who are today responsible for the good and honest development of public affairs would imitate this shining example of regal sentiment! Instead We see, and sometimes even in their ranks, the signs of tiring, of submission, of inactivity, which keep them from facing the problems of the present moment with firmness and perseverance, and so at times even permit events to go adrift, instead of arresting them with a wise and constructive action.

It is therefore necessary to mobilize all the vital strength which is today in reserve, to stimulate those who do not yet fully understand the dangerous psychological depression into which they have fallen. By this We do not intend to refer to any warlike intention, but only to the strength of the soul. . . . May Our imploring of the Queen of Heaven result in these men, who are failing in their responsibilities, overcoming their prostration and indolence, in this hour in which no one can permit himself one instant of rest, when in so many regions justice and liberty are suppressed, when truth is obscured by the activity of false propaganda, and the forces of evil appear to be unleashed well-nigh throughout the world.*

Is history repeating itself? It was and is a per-

* *Hibernia,* December, 1954.

tinent question to ask as we kneel here in the garden and pray, as we watch Judas advance and betray Him with a kiss, and His enemies gloatingly bind His hands and take Him prisoner.

The fruit of all this is sorrow with Christ Who is full of sorrow, and, indeed, it would not be too much to expect (as St. Ignatius would have us pray), that we should weep tears of grief in union with this great Sufferer "Who for my sins is going to His Sacred Passion." Nor should our sympathy stop short at mere feelings; it should be an urging to take deeply to heart the compelling words of the Holy Father, recognizing that in times like ours, "no one can permit himself one instant of rest."

CROSS AND CROWN

But the bitter chalice He presents to our lips is never without its admixture of sweetness. "The sufferings of the present time," wrote St. Paul, "are not worthy to be compared with the glory to come that will be revealed in us" (Rom. 8:18). And again: "For our present light affliction, which is for the moment, prepares for us an external weight of glory that is beyond all measure" (2 Cor. 4:17). His words came back to our minds as we walked home.

For we passed by the tomb which tradition points out as the one in which the body of Our Lady reposed during the brief period which elapsed between her death and her Assumption into heaven. Mary died in a room near the Cenacle, and her body was brought here by the apostles. This is now "The Church of the Dormition." It is in the charge of the German Benedictine Community of Beuron, and is enriched with many exquisite carvings from that world-famous school of art. On Mary's tomb there lies a wonderful oak statue, carved by the loving hands of the monks, showing Our Lady with both arms crossed on her breast in death. The bells that now peal from the tower remained lying on the ground for years after the church was built. The Moslems objected to them, but a group of pilgrims from Bavaria at last took the situation in hand. They erected the bells and there has been no further difficulty or disturbance about them.

The tomb is only a few minutes walk from Gethsemani. It spoke its message to us as we knelt around it. Our Blessed Lady suffered, even as her Son suffered, even as every friend of Christ must suffer. But suffering leads to glory. True, "there is no detour around the Hill of Calvary." But for Christ and for Mary, Calvary was not the end; only the beginning. The gloom of Gethsemani is transitory; the reward "exceeding great" is permanent. "If in this life only we have hope in Christ, we are of all men the most miserable."

A priest who heard we were going to the Holy Land had button-holed me one day. "If possible, what I'd like you to bring me would be some of the soil, just a little, from the garden of Gethsemani." We were told that a rule forbade us to pick anything off the trees, but said nothing about what we found on the ground. So I ventured to scoop out quite a respectable helping of the clay and collected four olives fallen already from their branches. Was he pleased when presented with the parcel? And when he came back a few times to explain how he had shared a portion of the treasure with one of his many friends?

Later, the Friars gave each of us a beautiful rosary, its beads made from the stones of the olives growing here, and a crucifix made from the wood. These treasures help to deepen the impressions and recall the feelings experienced in that silent night spent in one of the holiest places on earth.

But the very word "Gethsemani" stirs up sacred memories, showing us Him Who suffered there and reminding us that we knelt there where He had knelt, prayed where He had prayed, and tried to understand, despite the dullness of our minds, the undying message. For Gethsemani is a chapter in the greatest love story ever written, the love of God for souls. It is written in a language intelligible to every true lover, the language of sacrifice. It is written in red, the red ink of the Precious Blood, and the characters formed by that red ink remain ineffaceable.

17. *Cedron and Olivet*

Next morning our Mass at Gethsemani commemorated the Prayer of Christ. The setting for it was singularly apt. The words of the psalmist are placed on the lips of the Saviour here in agony. "My heart is troubled within me: and the fear of death is fallen upon me. Fear and trembling are come upon me: and darkness hath covered me" (Psalm 54:5–6). And the Collect cries out in earnest petition to Christ in His prayer: "O Lord Jesus Christ, Who in the garden didst teach us, by word and example, to pray in order to overcome dangerous temptations, graciously grant that we, always persevering in prayer, may merit to receive abundant fruit from it." "Watch and pray," the Postcommunion warns us, "that you enter not into temptation. The spirit indeed is willing but the flesh weak."

SEEING THE CITY

Another afternoon we crossed over the bed of the brook Cedron and climbed up the hill behind Gethsemani, till we came to the Mount of Olives. Halfway up is the church known as *Dominus Flevit.* It was here that Our Lord, wearied out by the persistent obstinacy of Jerusalem, sat down one day and "seeing the city, he wept over it, saying: If thou also hadst known and that in this thy day, the things that are to thy peace: but now they are hidden from thy eyes. For the days shall come upon thee: and thy enemies shall cast a trench about thee and compass thee round and straiten thee on every side, and beat thee flat to the ground, and thy children who are in thee. And they shall not leave in thee a stone upon a stone: because thou hast not known the time of thy visitation."

What an association of ideas must have been called up before His mind by the sight of the Temple on that day! This is the Temple where Our Lady was presented as a tiny child to God, and where she in turn, as a young mother, smilingly brought her own baby to be offered by the hands of the venerable Simeon. Alas, what a terribly abrupt ending there came to her gladness when she heard He was destined to be a sign to be contradicted, and that through her own soul a sword would pass! He had been here too as a little boy of twelve, remarkable for the fervor with which He took part in all the observances of the Jewish feast; but on the way home Mary and Joseph had lost Him, and sought Him sorrowing, and had finally found Him in the Temple, seated as a Master in the midst of the doctors, disputing with them and asking them questions. As a young man He had often preached there, in that Temple, and there was unction in His words and power to carry conviction, for He spoke as One having authority and not as the Scribes and Pharisees. Consumed with zeal for the glory of His Father's House He had one day made a whip and driven out the buyers and sellers, ordering them away and warning them they were not to make of this sacred place a den of traffic. All this and much more He might well have passed in review as He sits up here on the brow of the hill, and looks at it, Israel's glory and pride.

When He spoke this terrible prophecy the splendid Temple of the Jews lay there before Him, glistening in the sunlight. We looked down at the spot. The Temple is passed away and its glory is replaced by a mosque, the "Mosque of Omar." We had visited it a few days earlier. Before entering we had first either to take off our shoes or put on large loose shoes over our own, the object being, we were told, to avoid undue wear and tear on the rich carpets which cover the entire area of the floor. Judge of the magnificence of the decorations of this mosque from the fact that it cost the entire revenue of Egypt for four years to build it. For the Moslems it is the second holiest spot on earth, Mecca being the most sacred of all.

Right in the center is a large circular enclosure fenced in all the way round by a high trellis-work wall. A priest squatted near, tailor-wise, on the ground and kept all the time drawling out prayers. He nodded to us as we stood uncertainly at the door; so we came along and peered through the openings in the trellis. Inside is a large jutting-rock sacred alike to Christians, Jews, and Moslems, for it was on this rock, they believe, that Abraham prepared to sacrifice his son Isaac, at God's command, and would have done so had not an angel intervened at the last moment. God asked this sacrifice from His servant to test his faith; Catholics see in the incident a symbol of the Mass, wherein God's well-beloved son is mystically slain.

The place is a maze of mosaics, and stained-glass windows strike the eye everywhere. We could easily and pleasantly have spent a few hours here. The object that leaves you speechless with amazement is the huge dome which serves as a cupola for the rock, and has an interior consisting entirely of solid gold. We were not surprised to hear that wealthy Moslems consider it an honor to beautify the place regardless of expense.

WAILING WALL

Outside the mosque there is a large fountain where Moslems wash before they go in to pray. We saw some of them performing this ceremonial purification. They are called to prayer five times each day, and, from our place up at the *Dominus Flevit* we could hear the loud chants of those who had assembled. A smaller mosque lies to the south of the Mosque of Omar, famous principally because on one side is the Wailing Wall where the Jews used to stand and weep for the coming of the Messias and the restoration of Israel. But they do not weep there any more, all of them having left this part of the city to settle in the newly-formed Jewish State.

All this we now looked down upon from our place on the way to the Mount of Olives. One would not wish to have missed it. And all the time the thought would recur: "He was here. From this place He looked down on that same scene. Possibly the very spot where we were standing was touched by the feet of the God-Man." This hill, like the Sea of Galilee, is exactly what it was in His time. Human hands have not built upon it and there is comfort in the truth that it remains, and will remain, unchanged. "You haven't seen Jerusalem at all if you haven't seen it from here."

With this judgment of one of our party we all willingly agreed. Perspiration rolled off us and the blazing sun shrivelled us despite our elegant and effective Arab headgear, but it was worth the price.

MOUNT OF OLIVES

We had yet another stiff climb of another five hundred feet, till we reached the summit, the Mount of Olives, the scene of the Ascension of Our Lord into heaven. It is more than two thousand five hundred feet above sea level. Forty days after His Resurrection He had gathered the apostles together here and "he was lifted up before their eyes, and a cloud took him out of their sight" (Acts 1:9). And before He ascended, He gave one more last proof of the love of souls that had consumed Him all through His life. "All power in heaven and on earth," He declared, "has been given to me. Go, therefore, and make disciples of all nations, baptizing them in the name of the Father, and of the Son, and of the Holy Spirit. . . . And behold, I am with you all days, even unto the consummation of the world" (Matt. 28:18–20).

The rock upon which Our Lord stood before ascending into heaven is also pointed out. This is the rock that figures in the story of the pilgrimage of St.

Ignatius to Palestine. On the rock is the imprint of the feet of Christ, easy to discern with the eye and feel with the hand. The imprint of the left foot seems to be deeper than that of the right, giving you the impression that He would have pressed harder upon it. But there is no difficulty at all about tracing both.

St. Ignatius venerated these, as indeed he did every nook and corner that had any sort of connection with his "Master and Lord" whom he loved so ardently. But on leaving this mount, he did not feel altogether satisfied; he wanted to check again the precise position of the two imprints, so as to know the exact direction Our Lord was facing as He arose into the air. So he returned and bribed the guard of the place by presenting him with a penknife, to let him look a second time. Then once more he went away, but had not gone far down the mountain slope when another doubt occurred. So back again, and this time he parted with a pair of scissors for permission to examine more closely than before the impression made by the feet of Christ.

It was a little disappointing then, that our guide, for whose opinions all of us had learned to have the greatest respect, dismissed summarily the "imprint" part of the story. Of the site itself he has no doubt, and it was interesting to hear how certainty was reached. After the Ascension, the Acts of the Apostles relates that "they returned to Jerusalem from the mount called Olivet, which is near Jerusalem, a Sabbath day's journey" (Acts 1:12). This last detail serves to establish the place, for this reputed site of the Ascension is just within the distance which Jews were permitted to walk on the Sabbath. A thoughtful friend of mine had warned me, before leaving home, to make sure to provide myself in advance with a penknife and a pair of scissors. But it happened, as you see, that I did not need them.

The church belongs to the Moslems. Only on the eve of Ascension Thursday can the Franciscans use it to sing Matins and Lauds.

PALM SUNDAY

Bethphage, a village on the eastern side of the Mount of Olives, is the place where tradition says Our Lord mounted the ass to enter Jerusalem in triumph on Palm Sunday. He rode across this Cedron Valley at our feet, and through the Golden Gate, over there to our left. This gate is directly opposite the Franciscan Church at Gethsemani. The church faces the eastern wall of Jerusalem, and in that wall you have this gate. The Valley of Cedron intervenes, forming a deep gully, and the gate is on the ridge of the farther side of this gully, at a considerably greater elevation than the church.

In the time of the Crusaders the gate was opened on Palm Sundays and on the Feast of the Exaltation of the Cross, September 14. Years ago it was walled up by the Moslems, and it has remained so ever since. Nothing is there to remind you of its existence except the two semi-circles which were formerly the arches under which the processions used to walk, carrying palms and singing: "Hosanna, blessed is he that cometh in the name of the Lord!"

The Emperor Heraclius went through this gate in 629 bearing in triumph the true cross which he had won back from the Persians.

We could not resist the desire to turn in again for another visit to the garden of Gethsemani and the Church of All Nations. We felt we might not have another chance of being down in this direction, and for all of us this place was one of the most attractive in the Holy Land. On coming out we met a young Arab, aged about seventeen. He told us his elder brother had been killed in the recent disturbances and described the dire poverty in which himself and his mother were living. Of course we knew what he wanted. We found, when we made enquiries, that his sad tale was only too true and we were very glad we had tried to help him. He wasn't a Christian and spoke about "Jesus" in an impersonal sort of way that jarred a little. But there was no irreverence intended, and for him, poor lad, Jesus was just another historical religious figure, like Mohammed or Confucius.

On the way back to the city we called at a Convent of Carmelite nuns. On the marble walls of their church the words of the Our Father are done out in black and white slabs in thirty-five different languages. We were delighted to see one in Irish, and some of our party voted ours the most beautiful of all—and they weren't a bit prejudiced either! This is the Church of the Our Father, the traditional spot where Our Lord taught us that prayer.

13. *Via Dolorosa*

There is a tradition that after the death of Our Lord His Blessed Mother and the disciples used to go around and visit the different places where He had suffered. Even without this tradition, it is what we would expect to happen. If ever you go into a cemetery don't you see people tending the graves of those they loved in life and kneeling to pray for their souls? It is an unspeakable comfort to make this journey in Mary's blessed company, going over with her the actual route He had traversed, one of our many privileges during this memorable pilgrimage.

LOVE'S WAY

The sorrowful journey, the most sorrowful ever made, begins at the praetorium of Pilate and culminates on the Hill of Calvary. Where exactly the praetorium was is a much-discussed problem. Frankly, we were well satisfied to accept what is now the traditional spot and not delay over the arguments for and against. If most critics are agreed about it, it is sufficiently well established for our purpose. We began at the "Lithostrotos," the stone pavement on which Our Lord stood when He was sentenced, and we

152

passed under the "*Ecce Homo* Arch," where Pilate pointed Him out to the people who crowded the street below.

Ordinarily you would cover that distance from here to Calvary in a walk of about fifteen minutes. But it is certain that it must have taken Our Lord at least a full hour. Remember, He was in a condition of complete exhaustion, and the narrowness of the street, which at any time makes progress slow, increased the difficulty enormously when there was question of a whole procession moving along, and moving along with it three criminals each bearing an unwieldy cross on his shoulders. Further still, we have to keep in mind that Jerusalem was overcrowded at this particular period; strangers had poured in from everywhere to celebrate the Pasch.

There is a very deep and affecting reason for stressing these facts. Before we prepare to follow Him to Golgotha, it is worthwhile noting that by deliberate choice He has selected, for this humiliating journey, the one period in the year when it is going to cost Him most. Just as, at Bethlehem, He was born by preference during the brief span when the weather is harsh, so now He chooses for His death the time when, humanly speaking, its demands will be most exacting. For these great multitudes of people would constantly be getting in the way, breaking in on the procession from side streets and holding it up indefinitely. Keeping well before us the physical condition of the Saviour, it is not hard to imagine how these repeated delays added enormously to His sufferings.

The presence of so many in the town would have added, not only to His physical pains, but also to the humiliations He must endure. So many the more would be there to see and deride. It is our way, by nature, to cover up as much as possible anything that seems to humiliate us. We resent it if a chance remark of ours makes us look foolish and we hasten to try to correct it. We bridle up in self-defense the moment another misquotes us or shows us, in the presence of others, that what we have said is incorrect. All this alertness to cloak over our mistakes is evidence of the abundance of the pride that is in us. Now Jesus "humbled himself, becoming obedient unto death, even to death on a cross" (Phil. 2:8). His concern, therefore, is not to lessen, but rather to increase, the circumstances that will add to its difficulties. Love is like that.

A number of Jesuits were once taken prisoner. When

describing later on what they had suffered, they agreed that what cost most, was not being kept in prison or treated roughly and compelled to do hard labor on insufficient rations. What they found most humiliating was to be dragged round about in public procession and jeered at and booed by the spectators.

UNKNOWN GOD

Please do not cherish the illusion that any reverence was shown to us as we wedged our way through the dingy street from one Station to another. We found it difficult to keep together, for the crowds jostled us in different directions. Little boys would approach and stare and cry: Hello! Men sat at their doors with legs crossed, lazily smoking their hookahs, not interested, some of them dozing with head falling forward. Buying and selling went on apace—fish and bread and bales of cloth all around us—with prospective customers haggling over the price and prospective sellers all set to make a good deal.

Such indifference and ignorance shocked some of our party. Why, this is holy ground; this is the very route along which Jesus carried His cross. Have these thoughtless people no understanding of the sanctity of a spot which the pilgrim feels it is almost desecration to touch or walk upon? But on consideration how near to reality we find ourselves! On Good Friday when He stumbled along this pavement do you fancy there were found many to kneel and adore? A few women, indeed, did show compassion but to the vast majority Jesus Christ on that day was some unfortunate, serving the sentence which He richly deserved, in all probability, for His crimes. They just glanced, unseeing, in His direction for a moment, and then continued the conversation at the point where they had momentarily left off, or tried once more to beat down the salesman whose price was, or they pretended it was, exorbitant.

Others jeered at Him and grinned and pointed the finger of scorn and howled with derisive laughter whenever the poor Victim staggered and fell under His load. Some probably cursed Him, especially if the procession got in their way when they were in a hurry to some business that really mattered. A few seemed to be sorry for Him, and a lesser few still understood the stupendous truth that He was God, obeying the sentence of man that had condemned God to death. They will always be in a minority who fathom the mystery of the cross.

Every Friday the Franciscans lead a public procession along the Via Dolorosa and make the Stations of the Cross together with the people. We joined in, of course. Twelve or fifteen feet of rubble have been piled up on the road since first the Saviour walked this way. But of this you were scarcely conscious. Rather were you thrilled to hear, above the shouting and guffawing of the streets, the persuasively sweet tones of the Criminal, urging you to follow Him. "If anyone wishes to come after me, let him deny himself, and take up his cross, and follow me" (Matt. 16:24).

"AWAY WITH HIM"

If you walk up from Gethsemani and enter Jerusalem by the St. Stephen Gate, you will have no difficulty in finding the position of the First Station. It is on your right-hand side, just a few minutes past the gate. The Franciscan Fathers have a convent there, and in the compound and round about it, were enacted the tragic events that are associated with the first stages of this most sorrowful journey. The Sion Nuns, founded for the conversion of the Jews by Father Ratisbonne, formerly a Jew, are also quite near.

Here Jesus was scourged and mocked and crowned with thorns. Here He was exposed on the archway—pointed out to us—while Pilate stood by Him indicating Him to the Jews surging below. Here too stood the criminal Barabbas "who had been thrown into prison for a certain riot that had occurred in the city, and for murder" (Luke 23:19). They might have one of the two set free and Christ is rejected in favour of Barabbas. "So he [Pilate] released to them him who for murder and riot had been put in prison, for whom they were asking; but Jesus he delivered to their will" (Luke 23:25). Here was heard the terrifying curse they called down on their own heads: "His blood be on us and on our children" (Matt. 27:25). Here Pilate, shifting creature of compromise, had dipped his hands in a basin of water in sight of them all, and holding them dripping over the ledge of the balcony, had falsely asserted he was innocent of the blood of this just man.

"And bearing the cross for himself, he went forth to the place called the Skull, in Hebrew, Golgotha" (John 19:17). We saw Him take that cross; we helped to lift Him up when He collapsed under its weight; we met Mary His Mother at that corner, and a little farther on, Simon who took the cross for Him, and Veronica who wiped His face, and the group of women who wept in compassion. We edged our way through the bazaar and followed the Friars into the Church of the Holy Sepulchre to assist at the last five scenes of this never-to-be-forgotten journey, guiding ourselves from one spot to the next by footsteps traced in blood, His blood. "He is the first of an endless line of cross-bearers."

Our organizer had taken us around the Via Dolorosa on the morning before the regular Stations on Friday evening. Some of the scenes are marked only by a simple stone slab in the wall. Others have a small chapel, or a larger one—as in the case of the First Station outside the Franciscan Convent. Many of our good people were anxious to make this sorrowful journey again, along this route, so we went a second time by ourselves, a priest suggesting short meditations and prayers at each sacred halting-place.

St. John of the Cross once discovered in his little monastery at Duruelo a painting of Christ crucified. This he brought out and hung in the church in the hope that the sight of it might move the people to pray and stir up their love of Our Lord. Christ deigned to speak to His faithful servant: "John, you have done much for Me; what reward can I offer you for all your devotedness and zeal?" "Reward, Lord? One thing only do I beg—to be depised for Thy sake, to be entirely forgotten and ignored by men, and to suffer much for love of Thee!"

To the worldly-wise this is the height of foolishness. But, after treading in the Master's footsteps along the Via Dolorosa, one begins to understand a little better the heavenly wisdom of John's sublime answer. For one does learn wisdom here, a new wisdom, a new angle from which to view life. This wisdom is folly, the folly of the cross. It is this wisdom that transforms men, making them indeed fools, but "fools for Christ's sake." Love is extravagant; love does not slip in neatly and conform to convention; love cannot be weighed in the scales or measured out by the yard like a roll of cloth. To this day the cobblestones and the walls of the streets of the Via Dolorosa shout out that truth. Only those who are "fools for Christ's sake" have the wisdom to understand and the intelligence to deduce the logical conclusion.

19. *Where He Died*

The Church of the Holy Sepulchre was only ten minutes' walk from where we stayed in Jerusalem. It is right down in the heart of the present-day city. Within its four walls it embraces places the very thought of which stirs every Christian mind to awe and reverence. For this is where the Son of God was crucified, died, was buried, and rose again the third day.

Certain things about it you will not like, I'm afraid. We may as well mention them briefly and dismiss them. Your first shock will be the presence, at the entrance, of a Moslem guard who is always here on duty. Behind him is his couch where he lies down at night to sleep, within the precincts of this sanctuary! It is he who carries the key and opens and locks the door every morning and night. He is salaried by the different Christian Churches that share between them the possession of the Basilica.

SHOCKED?

Nor will you be impressed very favorably by the excessive and rather ponderous ornamentation on every side, and the lamps and candles burning everywhere in such profusion. We noticed that where the Friars have complete control—as, for example, at Nazareth or Mount Thabor—the shrine was free from this over-loading and the restraint a pleasant change.

Then there is the influx of sightseers. You will feel sorry for them, very sorry. They come and go continually, and this applies to the other Holy Places equally with this Church of the Holy Sepulchre. They are mere tourists, conducted around by a paid guide who duly recites his piece learned by rote, while his listeners try desperately hard to seem profoundly impressed. It is rather pathetic. For all they grasp of the significance of what he tells them, or he of what he is saying, he might as well be describing the wonders of the Acropolis or the Pyramids of Egypt. "This is the spot where the angel Gabriel spoke to the Virgin Mary. You are now looking at the site of the Birth of Christ. Before you lies the Tomb of Christ where He lay for three days before rising from the dead. If you switch on a light here and observe carefully you can see a portion of the pillar at which Christ was scourged. The other portion is in Rome."

And that is all! They look and stare and nod the head and gasp and consult their guide-book to check what he has said. Then turn on the heel, without a prayer, without an idea of the momentous meaning of it all. They can now go down town and purchase views of these places, and write to their friends that they are having a wonderful time. They have "done" the Holy Land!

Unless you have been prepared for it, you are going to be disedified by the jealousy and rivalry existing between the different sects. Greeks and Copts and Syrians and Latins have established rights here. All are Christians but nobody can help feeling that between them they are trying to tear Christ's seamless garment in shreds. Nor are you consoled when later on you learn that the Arabs, if urged by a Christian missionary to investigate the claims of the Church, will usually tell him derisively: "Please mend your own house first, and then it will be time enough to come along and convert us."

REALITY

The environment too you may find somewhat distracting. "Impossible to find a quiet place to pray in this church," one of our party complained. "To tell you the truth," another confided, "I'll be very glad to get back to Gardiner Street where I can say a decent prayer!" But these objections are not meant to be taken seriously, for after all isn't the whole pilgrimage a prayer?

Lastly, and perhaps above everything else, you will be horrified to observe how this superb basilica has been mutilated. A fire wrought havoc here two hundred and fifty years ago; and the restored edifice is ugly and confusing, a note of interrogation to the ordinary pilgrim, as he passes in through the door of the south transept, supported by an unsightly scaffolding for the past thirty years! He stands bewildered in the semi-darkness.

The late Archbishop of Cashel, Dr. Harty, once made this pilgrimage. When asked for his impressions when he came home, he invariably answered that he felt a sense of disappointment. If you have read thus far you will surmise why. But, admitting the defects we have indicated, it still remains true that if it is reality you want, you have, beyond all question, come to the one place on earth where, more than any other, you are certainly going to find it.

When you have stood for a minute or two inside and your eyes have grown accustomed to the dim light, turn your head and look to the right. A flight of stairs is just beside you. Climb up those stone steps, as thousands of pilgrims have climbed before you; indeed you will notice that the surface is quite worn away as a result. When you reach the top—there are about forty steps in the flight—halt and recollect yourself; join both hands, perhaps instinctively, and draw near, very slowly and reverently, to that altar there in front of you. You are standing on the Hill of Calvary. It is established beyond doubt that this is the place where the cross was lifted up with the Saviour of the world nailed to it.

Black out every other memory. Forget the elements of human strife and human emulation going on down below; prescind from the lamps and the ornaments and the disfigured basilica. What do such things matter, after all, when you are here face to face with reality? Magdalene knelt in this spot at His bleeding feet. Our Lady stood here, at your right, and St. John beside her. You can even place your hand, if reverence does not overawe you, on the very socket into which the cross of Christ was jolted.

CONSUMMATUM

It was here He spoke those seven last words upon which you often pondered; perhaps heard them preached on Good Friday in your own parish. Here

He hung for three hours while darkness covered the whole earth. Here He cried out with a loud voice; this is the place through which His last prayer sent out its echo: "It is consummated" (John 19:30). "Father, into thy hands I commend my spirit" (Luke 23:46). Just beside where you are standing, the soldier had stood after the death, and, taking steady aim, had thrust the spear forward to pierce His side and wound the Sacred Heart of Christ. And blood and water issued forth, and flowed down along by the side of that rock upon which your eyes are now privileged to gaze.

To come here on the following morning and celebrate Mass or assist at it, is an experience that shakes the soul to its very foundations. All priests offering the Holy Sacrifice up here say the Mass of the Holy Cross, or the Mass of the Passion. "It behooveth us to glory in the cross of Our Lord Jesus Christ, in which is our salvation, our life, and our resurrection; through which we are saved and set free. . . . He humbled himself, becoming obedient unto death, even to the death of the cross; for which cause also God hath exalted him, and hath given him a name that is above every other name" (Phil. 2:8–9). "What are these wounds in the midst of thy hands? With these was I wounded in the house of them that loved me." These few excerpts suggest how beautifully appropriate are these Masses in such a setting.

Mass here is the King's secret, too sacred to be discussed, its fitting place being the innermost recesses of each one's soul.

TOMB OF CHRIST

When finally His head fell forward in death, Joseph of Arimathea and Nicodemus set ladders by the cross, took hammers, and climbed to drive out the nails. Mary stood here close to you, waiting to take into her eager embrace that body, sadly disfigured, while the sword of sorrow, foretold by Simeon, pierced her heart. Reverently the two men lowered that sacred burden, and brought it down that slope which you ascended by the stairs a while ago, until they reached the Stone of Unction where they laid it out preparatory to anointing it for burial. This Stone still lies in the Church of the Holy Sepulchre, flat on the ground right in front of you after you come in. It is a large rectangular slab of marble and Mary and the women and Joseph and Nicodemus all helped here to wash the body and embalm it before placing it in the tomb. They worked in haste, for the Law enjoined that everyone should be within doors before sundown. Having finished all that love could provide in the short space allowed them, they bore it across to the grave, "wrapped in fine linen and laid Him in a sepulchre that was hewed in stone, wherein never yet any man had been laid" (Luke 23:53).

It was provided by the charity of Nicodemus. Christ's mother was too poor to pay for anything very grand. Her divine Son was buried in what might be called a pauper's grave. His whole life is of a piece, for He was born in a cave; in His public life He had nowhere to lay His head, a man of no fixed abode; and now in death He depends on the goodwill of a kind-hearted man to give Him a place where His lifeless body may repose.

The tomb occupies a prominent position in the church and it is the first object that attracts your attention. Calvary, you remember, is on your right after you come in; the tomb is on your left. Calvary is elevated to a height of about fifty feet; the tomb is on the ground floor, on a level with the surface surrounding the building outside. As the evangelists described it, it is hewn out of the solid rock, reminding you of the caves similarly hewn at Bethlehem and at St. Joseph's house in Nazareth,

Jerusalem

Herzl Street in modern Jerusalem

It consists of two apartments, the first one comparatively large, where the angel sat on Easter morning and greeted the holy women. The inner room is much smaller and you can manage to get in only by bending very low, and keeping carefully to the injunction to "mind your head." Everyone kneels here; everyone prays here. The body of the dead Christ rested in this place from Good Friday evening till Easter Sunday. An altar is erected over the exact spot, the altar-table of marble, and by the great courtesy of the Franciscan Fathers it was the author's privilege to sing a Solemn High Mass here one morning. The little enclosure is barely large enough to permit the presence of three priests. During the Gloria and Credo we doubled ourselves up and went out into the main portion of the church to sit down. All the people heard the Mass from here and the Friars sang, accompanying a choir of little Arab boys.

During this High Mass the Copts were also having a Mass of their own. Their altar was just behind ours, and right lustily did they sing. Maybe we were uncharitable, but you could scarcely help feeling that they were trying to drown us, and to impress us, and tell us "where we got off!" Their Mass was somewhat longer than ours, so after we had finished I wandered around to see. A priest was incensing the altar and all its precincts. He had a long bluish chasuble with silver ornamentation, reaching to his ankles. On his head he wore what I can only call a sort of biretta, such as you see in pictures of priests in the Old Testament, close-fitting and resembling a boat in shape. While he was swinging the censer—and he kept swinging for a long time, making sure to omit no tiny corner—he chanted alternately with the choir. It was a pleasant tune, but too violent, we thought.

One confesses to a feeling of helplessness and to a sense of futility as one tries to chronicle the events of these wonderful days. The mere external happenings can be written down and preserved and read about. Immeasurably more important is the effect on mind and heart. This cannot be put into words, and even if it could, perhaps should not be.

20. *L'Envoi*

Our last day on this holy ground. After Mass at the ruins of the synagogue in Capharnaum we drove to the Mount of Beatitudes overlooking the Sea of Galilee. Bags were packed and stowed on our bus before we sat down to lunch. It was Friday, and we had fish called "*mustch*," which, they told us, is of the same family as the fish out of whose mouth St. Peter took the two staters. Our Lord had sent him down to this sea and told him to cast in his line, and open the mouth of the first fish he caught. He did, and found the two pieces of money with which to pay the tax. Perhaps that was why the "*mustch*" were served to us "heads and all!"

A final short visit to the Blessed Sacrament and then goodbye to the nuns and all aboard. We looked wistfully, for the last time, at the grandeur of the scene. As the bus moved along we pointed out to each other Capharnaum, Tiberias, Magdala, the hills around the lake, each with its own memories and message. We kept a lookout for the lake itself, whenever we had the chance, lying in its great loveliness beneath.

MOUNT CARMEL

All this we had now to leave behind us and we left it with a feeling of nostalgia, though the remembrance of it will always be an inspiration. We were bound for Haifa, on the Mediterranean coast, and for Mount Carmel, austere and majestic, sanctified by the prayers and penances of the prophet Elias, Father of the Carmelites, and by his sons who live up there today. We strained to get a final glimpse of Nazareth en route, a few miles over there to our left.

The monastery of Mount Carmel, two miles outside Haifa, is situated at a height of nearly five hundred feet. We were welcomed by Father Elias, the Jewish convert, formerly Dr. John Friedman. The church is built on a great quadrangle and we knelt at the grotto where tradition says the prophet used to live and spend so much of his time in prayer. It was not difficult to imagine him, for inside is a fine life-size statue of Elias, with beard reaching to his breast, seated at a table with quill pen in hand. Over the cave is the high altar surmounted by a statue of Our Lady of Mount Carmel. We kept the Brother in the repository busy as many of us had Carmelite friends and wanted to send cards from this place so dear to every son and daughter of Elias.

The Carmelite apostolate is, in the main, one of prayer and penance. Here on this high mountain apart, these monks offer incessantly to God their dedicated lives for the conversion of Israel, mindful of that profound truth emphasized by St. John of the Cross that "one single act of pure love is of more benefit to the Church than all other works put together." Obviously this is not by any means to depreciate the value of external labors but only to put them in correct focus, for the exterior apostolate is certain to be barren unless it be the flowering of the interior life. It can never be a substitute for prayer and penance.

TEL AVIV

Most of the country is under tillage; everywhere you saw the sprays supplied by the artificial irrigation which transforms this desert into arable land. The crops were still green, as there are two harvests each year. Coming down from Carmel we had a splendid view of Haifa, the harbor, and a vast stretch of the Mediterranean. Our guide proudly showed us the oil refineries, and grew lyrical in his praise of the growth of the town and of Israel generally. The Jews are proud of what they have to show and they have sweated and toiled in producing it. If reports be true the dollars have poured in by the million from Jews the world over.

Tired but happy we got into Tel Aviv that evening. At once you sensed that you were back in another world. This is a different atmosphere, the workaday world where the things of the spirit are unknown, where men's interest is in money and a good time. What first caught our attention was the cinema hoardings and their modern "flash" films, advertised all over the place. For weeks we had not seen a film or advertisement, and we came back with a jolt to electric lights and screaming headlines and the "situations" depicted. Forty-five years ago a start was made to build this city. The idea at first was to make it an extension of Jaffa which lies to the south. Actually what has happened is that in that brief period Tel Aviv has entirely eclipsed Jaffa. Jaffa is now a mere suburb. Tel Aviv now boasts four hundred and fifty thousand inhabitants. It is a spacious, well-planned, modern city, with skyscrapers, cinemas and theaters, first-class hotels, excellent bus and train services, and everything you associate in your mind with progressiveness in this age of progress. But frankly, I'm afraid many of us were not enthusiastic. Tel Aviv was anti-climax.

JAFFA

Next morning, Sunday, we drove out to Jaffa for Mass and Holy Communion. This is the town where St. Peter, while living in the house of Simon the tanner, had a vision from heaven that foreshadowed the preaching of the Gospel to the Gentiles—to us. Here is Peter's own account: "I was praying in the city of Joppa, and while in ecstasy I had a vision, a certain vessel coming down something like a great sheet, let down from heaven by its four corners, and it came right down to me. And gazing upon it, I began to observe, and I saw the four-footed creatures of the earth, and the wild beasts and the creeping things, and the birds of the air. And I also heard a voice saying to me, 'Arise, Peter, kill and eat.' And I said, 'By no means, Lord, for nothing common or unclean has ever entered my mouth.' But the voice answered a second time, 'What God has cleansed, do not thou call common'" (Acts 11:5–10).

It was here too that Peter raised to life the widow Tabitha, who "had devoted herself to good works and acts of charity. . . . They took him [Peter] to the upper room. . . . But Peter . . . knelt down and prayed; and turning to the body, he said, 'Tabitha, arise' " (Acts 9:36–40).

In the sacristy an Irish nun stood to welcome us, only wishing we could stay longer and talk about Ireland. But we had to press forward. Out to the airport where the plane had been "docked" during all our time in Palestine, and once more on board. We stopped at Athens, Naples, Marseilles, and Collinstown. The diary open before me speaks of the glorious day at Naples where we sat in sunshine over the bay on November 15. It records the one really unpleasant half-hour we had throughout the entire pilgrimage, when the plane ran into distinctly rough weather and anything might have happened. We thanked God fervently that nothing did. "And did you make an Act of Contrition?" a priest asked later when listening to this description. "Never thought of it, Father," was the shameful confession we had to make. We went to bed at Marseilles and, after some difficulty, found a church in the morning in which to say Mass.

On that night, about seven o'clock, we reached the Dublin airport at Collinstown. Welcome home! It was good to hear it.

OVER THERE

Before we finally dispersed we got together to pay a well-deserved tribute of gratitude and appreciation to our travel agent for his unfailing efficiency and courtesy at all times. While we were at Nazareth we were assured that tourists on conducted tours were often allotted not more than half an hour on their schedule for a visit to that town! On our pilgrimage we reached Nazareth at two o'clock one afternoon, spent the rest of the day there and had Mass on the following morning. This is one instance of the satisfactory manner in which every detail was planned for us.

We were also deeply indebted to the Franciscan Fathers and Brothers, custodians of the Holy Land, for guiding us around, arranging for us to say Mass at all the sacred places, planning our Holy Hour, Way of the Cross, and other devotions. Through their courtesy we had the privilege of an audience with the Patriarch of Jerusalem, also a Franciscan, and he expressed the hope that many other Irish pilgrims would follow us out here. On our last day in Jordan there was a reception, a very pleasant function indeed, at the Franciscan convent, during which each of us was presented with precious souvenirs.

In Israel our official guide was Father Jean Roger, an Assumptionist Augustinian, and in Jordan Mr. Tawfig Morcos, a staunch Arab Catholic. By no stretch of the imagination could you regard either of them as the mere official, giving out information in parrot fashion. Both these men knew these Sacred Places most intimately and it was clear too that they loved and reverenced every inch of this holy ground. Their presence with us was a pillar of light not by night only but throughout the day as well. They know we are thankful.

You might meet them sometime, out there. I hope so.

A NOTE ON THE TYPE

IN WHICH THIS BOOK WAS SET

This book has been set in Electra, a type face created in 1935 by W. A. Dwiggins, the well-known Boston artist. This type falls within the "modern" family of type styles, but was drawn to avoid the extreme contrast between "thick and thin" elements that marks most "modern" type faces. The design is not based upon any traditional model, and is not an attempt to revive or to reconstruct any historic type. Since its birth, Electra has met with success because of its easy-to-read quality. This book was composed and printed by the York Composition Company, Inc., of York, and bound by Moore and Company of Baltimore. The design and typography of this book are by Howard N. King.